Voice Gym Book
"Get to know your Voice"
by
Angela Caine
Voicegym

www.voicegym.co.uk

Fourth Edition, published April 2014 by VoiceGym Ltd.
ISBN 978-0-9553799-7-0

Copyright © 2003 - 2014, A Caine and C Lewis.
Copyright © 2014, VoiceGym Ltd., all rights reserved

This document is copyright of "VoiceGym Ltd". Any redistribution or reproduction of part or all of the contents in any form is prohibited other than the following:
- you may print or download to a local hard disk extracts for your personal and non-commercial use only
- you may copy the content to individual third parties for their personal use, but only if you acknowledge VoiceGym as the source of the material

You may not, except with our express written permission, distribute or commercially exploit the content. Nor may you transmit it or store it in any other website or other form of electronic retrieval system.

Reasonable effort has been made to obtain permission for reproduction of all photographs and diagrams. Where sources could not be found it is hoped that the educational nature of this project, together with credits and references in the bibliography, will suffice.

Acknowledgements

"In order to advise them, I was often compelled to broaden my scientific horizons by going beyond my immediate areas of expertise": *Edmund S. Crelin, PhD DSc, writing about his students in the Departments of Surgery, Orthopaedics and Rehabilitation, Yale University School of Medicine.*

Edmund Crelin's work first encouraged me to step beyond the teaching of singing to search for the recovery of my voice. However, I would never have heard of him or his splendid book if it were not for Sir Jonathon Miller's television Series 'Origins' in the seventies.

The desire to question received wisdom must come from my father, who was an unarmed dispatch rider and ambulance driver in the 1914-18 'Great War for Civilisation' believing it to be more useful than going to prison for his beliefs. Without my mother's desire to 'sing and dance on the stage', frustrated by a Victorian father, my introduction to music may not have been as varied and as much fun as it was.

Alex Boswell, teacher of English and German at Rhyl Grammar School fired my love of language and sowed the seed of the discovery, fifty years later, that language rhythm is the fundamental of music, song and dance.

Alred Fonder BA. DDS, a pioneer of functional orthodontics and whole body dentistry, was the first of many dentists and orthodontists to influence my thinking. Among them are Mike Fennell, Peter Watt, Helen Jones, John Gane and Wojciech Tarnowski.

Physiotherapist Elizabeth Cardew was inspirational when I was searching for the links between body and voice and subsequently the clinical disciplines of Cranial Osteopathy and SOT Chiropractic have made a significant contribution to the structural alignment information and treatment that has put many voices back into performance through Tim Oxbrow, Jonathon Howat, Stephen Williams, Pam Elkins and Caroline Laurence. Sarah Dunlop, Pilates Teacher working with UK Olympic sailors, surfers and divers has supplied the 'edge' to these performers. Tony Buzan convinced me many years ago of the importance of the right brain in learning.

Don Burton, physiotherapist and Alexander Teacher, who trained me in the Alexander technique, died in 1998 and so will never know that my head failed to go 'up and forward' because I had lost so many back teeth to inappropriate dentistry (see Chapter 7- *Jaws and Teeth*). His teaching of functional anatomy, as opposed to 'dead anatomy' freed me to experiment with balance and stretch.

Without Chris Lewis, my husband, editor, technical adviser, encouragement and support, this book would never have happened. We all dedicate this book to everyone who has ever wanted a better voice. Angela Caine, July 2006

Forward

By Alexander Evans BA(Hons)

I first met Angela in the mid 90's as a student at Southampton University. I became one of the first in a pilot study to see what effects Orthodontic and Chiropractic work would have on the voice. At the age of 18 I had lost my ability to sing though there was nothing pathologically wrong with the voice it became clear throughout the study that the way to recovery from my vocal problems was to explore what these professions could do for me and others with similar problems. Angela taught a number of students from the University, many who went under similar treatment. We embarked on a study that was to continue beyond University where I studied alongside my colleague Simone Laraway at the Voice Workshop, to become Voice Gym instructors. After University the three of us continued to teach and run workshops together and further developed the programmes that became VoiceGym, and Early VoiceGym.

Once I had become stable enough, I began to embark on a career as a professional Singer, Actor and Musician which has taken me across three continents singing both opera and music theatre, on tours and into London's West End: a testament to the power of Angela's work and the work of her associated clinicians.

Though many steps have been made there is still naivety amongst the singing profession in ignoring the dangers of functional anatomy, dentistry and skeletal misalignment. As Angela wrote in my first music score, 'Beware the chiefs! Stick close to the Indians'."

Since the passing of Angela in 2011 Simone and myself continue to teach the programmes and are dedicated to keep developing VoiceGym and Early VoiceGym.

The programmes are a valuable tool for singers, actors, musicians or for any new to singing or need confidence in public speaking and can be used as a part of a daily warm up routine, just by picking a selection of exercises that are best suited to your needs.

They also provide a great way of educating sports professionals / coaches (and vocal coaches) in the pitfalls of teaching cortical control breathing, and can provide an imaginative and fun way of adding voice to any daily work out regime.

Finally (and from first-hand experience!) they are an essential part of any dental / orthodontic treatment, providing a set of whole body exercises to improve the posture, flexibility and health of the entire vocal / breathing suspension and can speed up and help maintain orthodontic treatment in children and adults...

They are designed to be fun so don't over think... just play, and as Angela once said "Mindless repetition never achieves anything, and no one ever learns anything unless it is fun"

The programmes are a valuable tool for singers, actors, musicians or for any new to singing or need confidence in public speaking and can be used as a part of a daily warm up routine, just by picking a selection of exercises that are best suited to your needs. They also provide a great way of educating sports professionals / coaches (and vocal coaches) in the pitfalls of teaching cortical control breathing, and can provide an imaginative and fun way of adding voice to any daily work out regime.

Contents

Introduction 6

1. Practical Working Models 9
2. Early Development - Infancy 18
3. Early Development - Childhood 31
4. The Adult Voice 39
5. Breathing, the Myths and the Mischief 47
6. The importance of Tongue Position 68
7. Face Muscles 76
8. Balance and Posture 86
9. Jaws and Teeth 102
10. Words and Rhythm 127
11. A Professional Voice for Life 147

Appendix 166

Useful Contacts 169

Bibliography and References 171

Glossary 174

Introduction

The good use of the voice is such a basic life skill that one wonders why it eludes so many people. We are born with singing, the primary function of the voice, and all the potential for continued development. We learn language from those around us. The voice is an integral part of the breathing system so the fact that we are living and breathing confirms that we have the means to voice development. You would think one only had to grow up with the need to communicate for natural development to take place. Yet my experience is that all this potential gets whittled away throughout childhood, school and beyond and rarely matures into the adult voice that is our natural inheritance.

Anyone can be suffering from an undesirable voice but unless it becomes a real threat to professional life, or keeps disappearing, improvement is unlikely to be considered. When I am 'discovered' in trains, aeroplanes, ferries and other places where you are unlikely to meet this person again people tell me about their voices in the same hushed tones in which they would admit to a secret sin. The man who put up my garden fence heard someone singing in the house and spent half an hour of his lunch break (and mine!) telling me how much he had always wanted to sing,

Microphones are everywhere, not just as part of the trappings of music culture, but the headmaster has one to speak to the school, the vicar to the congregation and likewise every public hall is wired for sound. At public meetings someone continuously scurries from person to person in the audience, while we all wait to hear the question. Unfortunately making sound louder does not also make it clearer.

If you are not satisfied with the way you look there are many ways to do something about it. You can tackle the body with exercise, change your diet, live better, or with enough money you can change the exterior image with a good designer 'fix'.

To get help with your voice you generally have to already have a voice that is considered worth helping. There are speech lessons for those who are already good at speaking and singing lessons for those who can sing.

This is a "Catch 22" situation. If your voice gets noticed, you are given the opportunity and encouragement to use it. That opportunity probably helps to get it noticed some more and you develop the idea that your voice is worth attention. But how do you get to Square 1? How do you get the voice that *you* like and you use with enough confidence to get it noticed in the first place? What is the nutrition necessary for developing a good voice?

I believe the information is all around us, but it is in so many different places, books and clinical disciplines that it is difficult to find. It is in singing, language, early development, osteopathy, chiropractic, dentistry, neurology, pathology, - in fact in every discipline, everywhere you look. When you do find it there are conflicting messages because the people who are giving the different messages never meet to thrash out their differences. The fragmentation of this information and the division of the voice into singing and speech, which is then subdivided into speech training and speech therapy, has caused a stalemate in the natural development of a good voice that required a lifetime to put it all together.

Well, I just happened to have a lifetime to do just that.

I have written this Book to check out and then consolidate all the fragmented information on voice into one place so that it is available to everyone wherever and whenever they want to begin to improve their voice, and because this information on voice has been cross referred in many different disciplines, it actually works.

When you have read it, if you are inspired to approach the development of your voice in a way more in tune with twenty first century thinking you might consider taking on the VoiceGym Voice-and-Body Exercise programme, or introducing Early VoiceGym to your children under eight. Both are available from www.voicegym.co.uk

VoiceGym is particularly helpful to those who:
- Had a poor vocal beginning from which they would like to escape. It is for the academic child who sat, sat and sat studying for ten years at school and four or even five years at University and is now a lecturer, a doctor, a teacher, or a lawyer, and in all of those years there has been no help to develop the voice that is so necessary in a life dealing with people.
- Have been told they can't sing by someone who knew nothing about it, but they were so little and emotionally fragile from having to face the singing out that the experience has never left them. They can remember the colour of the dress the teacher wore and which lesson it was on which day. Maybe they were 6 years old and now they are sixty,

but it does not go away and has prevented their singing of 'Away in a Manger' every Christmas since.

- Have a terror of being asked to read in public because they never really conquered reading aloud. They just managed to get by in school by avoiding drama, poetry, literature, etc. However, they have now moved up the professional ladder and every meeting is a nightmare, where minutes or reports have to be read aloud. One day it will be them.
- Speak English as a second language and who need to acquire the speech rhythm and pitch pattern of English so they can be more easily understood. English is now the language of international commerce, business, engineering and science.
- Already sing or speak well, but who want to know why they do and how they do, so they feel more secure. It is a good maintenance system.

Early VoiceGym is for parents and teachers of 5-8 year olds

Singing and speech are both developed for maximum potential by playing voice games and singing: the bonus is a confident articulate child.

Above all I want to put 'play' back into playing the musical instrument we call the voice. This is the primary musical instrument from which all others developed! Singing has become a potentially fearful thing to do: associated with making a fool of yourself, being inadequate, not being good enough to sing the songs. The person listening to you expressing your views or giving a presentation is so often seen as a critic, a judge, rather than someone receiving a rare gift – a bit of you. There is another way to learn to use your voice that is empowering.

1. Practical Working Models

The word 'Anatomy' means to cut up, to dissect. Unless you have the big picture to begin with, cutting up into bits can get you completely lost in the detail. At the end of the day how do you ever put the bits back together so that you understand the whole system?

I have begun with some models that show that the dynamic body is based on a series of springs. You can come back to these when you lose the plot elsewhere in the book. Everyone's brain works differently. Find the level of information in this book that your brain responds to and gradually try to access other levels. When you can't understand what I am trying to explain, come back to these simple models.

Never assume that the lack of understanding is down to you. It is my job to make things clear. After all, I am the teacher, the specialist in my subject. If I can't make it clear, it's not your fault, but mine. You have my email...

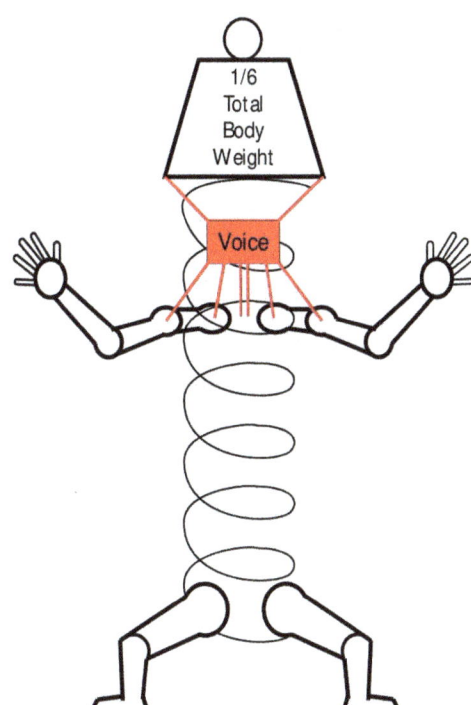

The human body is supported on a huge spring: the spine.

This spring is stimulated by the feet meeting the ground at the bottom and the weight of the head at the other end.

The voice and breathing system is suspended from underneath the head and connected down on to the shoulder girdle and sternum,

The suspension operates in every direction to allow for all the movement of spine, head, and arms.

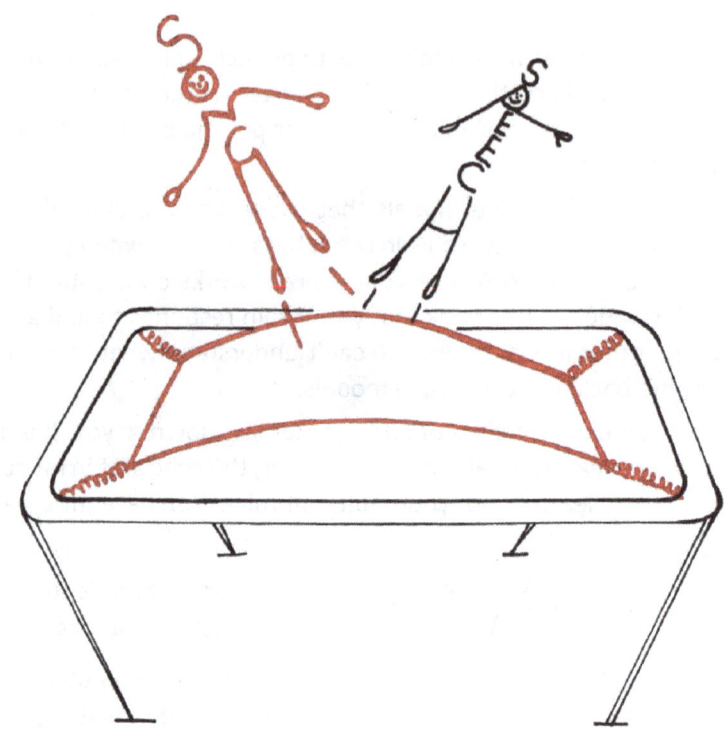

The Vocal Trampoline

The spring action that is the basis of everything we do is repeated in the action of the voice.

Speech and singing can operate with such enormous variety of pitch, colour and resonance because of the spring in the whole voice suspension.

Think of the mat above as being the larynx and the springs as the muscles connecting the larynx to the frame.

The frame is your skeletal structure. Everything works on down spring and rebound.

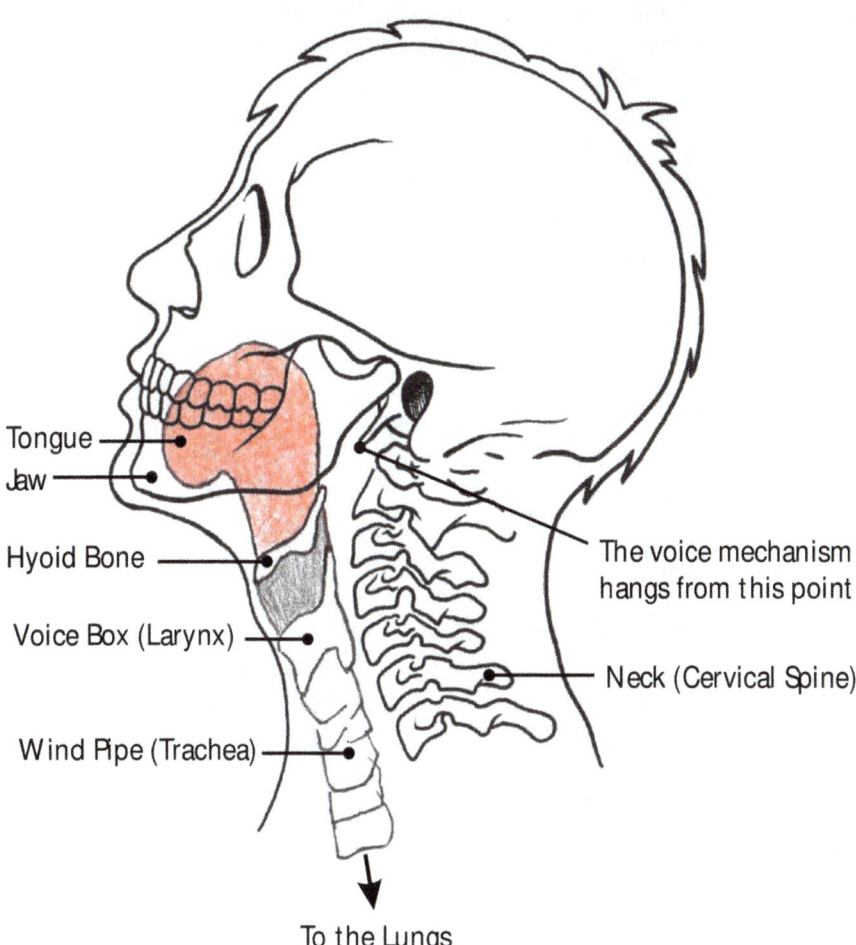

Where is the mechanism of breathing / voice?

Begin with this model so that you get used to the order of things.

This is the top of the system. You will find a more detailed diagram of the same area on page 44. Compare them.

The next four diagrams illustrate six important springs. Most muscles run vertically. These muscles run horizontally. They add spring and rebound to all physical activities, including breathing and voice. Here are three of them.

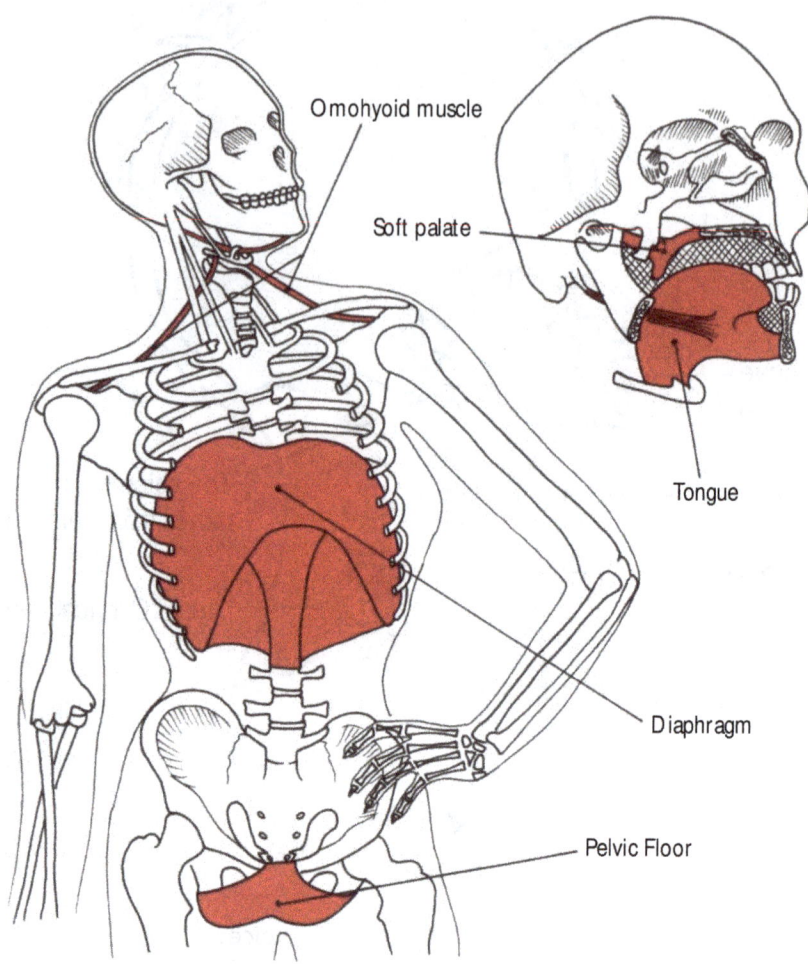

The **Diaphragm** is the central, and strongest, spring, but by no means the only one. The **Pelvic floor,** another important spring, plays an important role in the quality of the voice

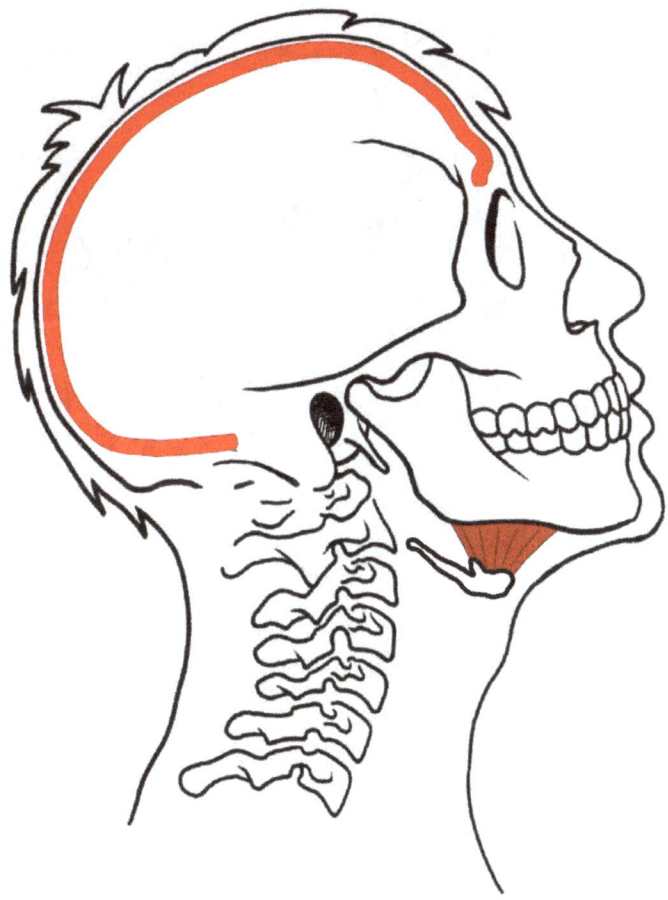

Two More Lateral Springs

The elastic membrane that encloses the brain – the **Dura mater** – is the top spring of the body see Chapter 2 - *Early Development - infancy*.

Mylohyoid – the muscle that forms the floor of the mouth, below the tongue and inserts into the hyoid bone - is another.

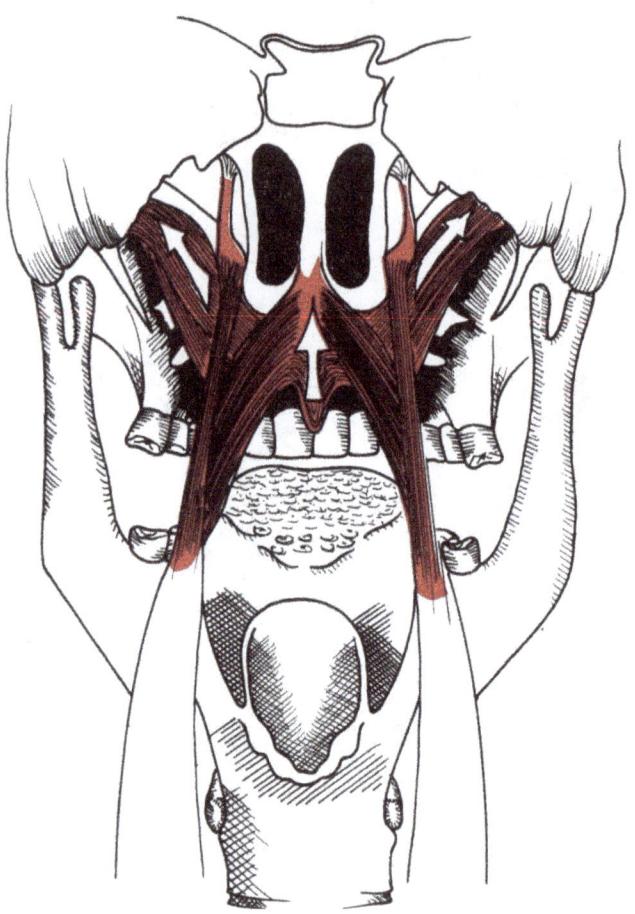

The Soft Palate, another spring

Imagine that you are standing on a ledge at the very back of your mouth. The teeth are apart and you can see out through them across the top surface of your tongue. The hole in front leads into your larynx. The two black holes are the inside of your nose Everything red is your soft palate and the arrows show that it can be pulled up vertically and also outwards diagonally. Lift your soft palate and pull it sideways at the same time. This lifts and widens the upper part of the face.

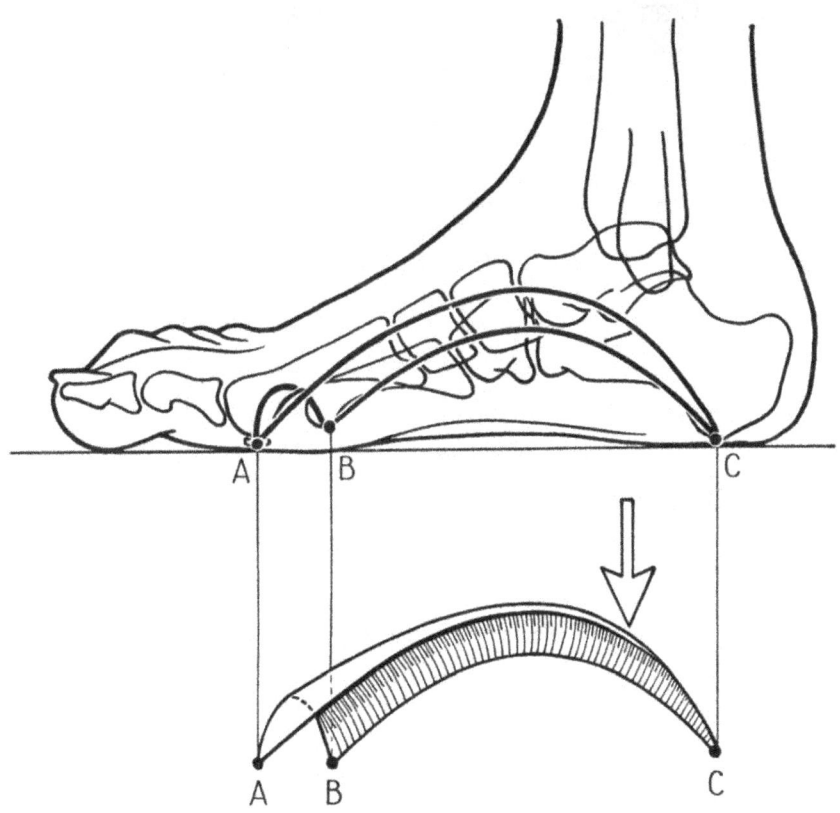

The Foot Spring (After Kapandji,1974)

Maybe this is the most important spring of all. We stand on three points of the foot and the three arches that meet at those three points determine the balance of the upright biped. The weight bearing of the triangles in both feet – the plantar mechanism – are a major influence on the rhythm and co-ordination of all the other five springs.

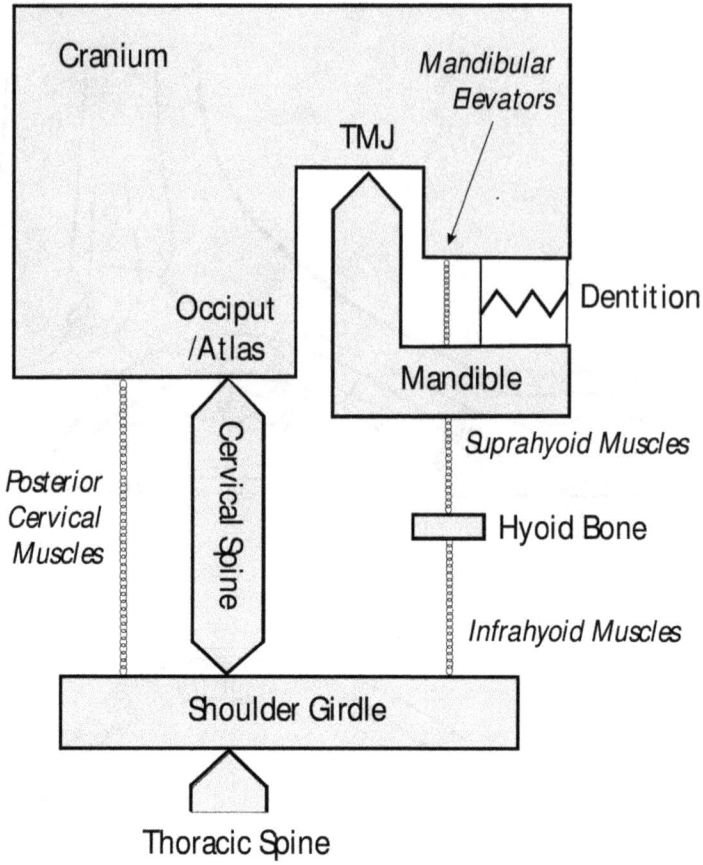

This is a model drawn by Fonder (1990), to show the relationship between head, neck and shoulder girdle.

This illustrates the role of the dentition in maintaining the balance between extension (the posterior muscle system) and flexion (the anterior muscle system).

Influence of the Right Brain

Add imagination and play, and the poor dull voice on the left becomes the magnificent butterfly on the right.

The six springs in descending order:
1. The Dura Mater encasing the brain
2. The Soft Palate
3. The Mylohyoid Muscle from Mandible to Hyoid
4. The Central Diaphragm
5. The Pelvic Floor
6. The Plantar Mechanism in the feet

Stand in front of a mirror and locate all of these springs on your self.

A diaphragm is a flexible partition that can regulate the pressure of the two areas it separates. All of these springs can be said to function as diaphragms, so it is important not to become fixated by the work of the central diaphragm. Rhythm, in you and in the music you play, is dependant upon the coordinated function of all of them. In a voice of quality all are strong

What is generally referred to as '*the* Diaphragm' is only a part of this rhythmic system and isolating its action, in either your belief system or your exercise, can severely limit rhythmic response (see Chapter 8 - *Balance and Posture*).

2. Early Development - Infancy

Listening to Mother

The baby hears mother's voice first, whenever she speaks and sings throughout pregnancy, through the bone conduction and resonance of her body spaces. Everyone in the family plays some part in giving the child's voice a good start but no-one has the unique opportunity to influence the voice of this child *for life* as does the mother.

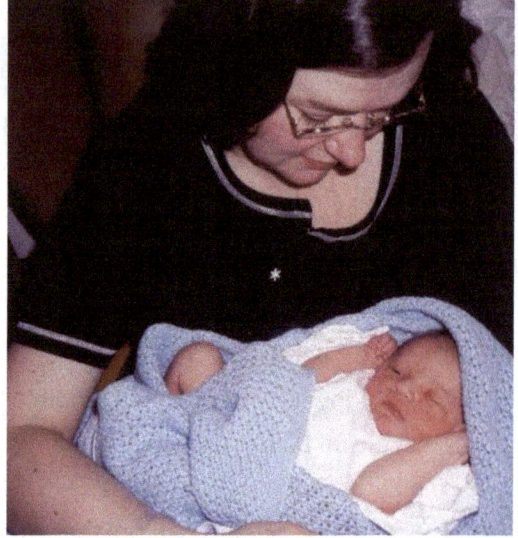

Bonding is everything

Hearing and listening begin early. The Mother becomes the role model for the child's voice at about two months into pregnancy. If a strong bond is formed at this stage, the ear/voice relationship is likely to remain strong throughout life, aiding other forms of listening and through that, concentration. Listening is the fundamental tool for *all* learning as well as for language, music and communication skills. Mothers are the primary role model and should be encouraged, during pregnancy, to sing and talk to their babies as much as possible – certainly every day.

Birth and singing

Michel Odent (1984), a French gynaecologist, first introduced underwater birthing. He encouraged the patients in his own clinic to sing regularly all the way through pregnancy. He found that singing encouraged flexibility and control of the pelvic muscles and allowed the mother to follow more accurately the instructions of 'no push yet' and OK, Push Now'. Mothers were encouraged to sing throughout the strong contractions so that they did not interfere with the natural enlargement of the pelvis through tensing abdominal muscles against it. African midwives in remote areas still sing with their patients to help labour pains. Singing can be a relaxing and loving part of antenatal care for both mother and baby (see 'Active Birth Centre' in Useful Contacts).

When the natural mother has to be replaced by a mother figure, the development of listening and communicating skills can continue in the close bonding during feeding and caring for the baby, provided that mother figure talks and sings to her baby. Although the baby cannot outwardly talk back or copy the singing, the 'talk back' and copying systems are being processed all the same.

A strong bond is formed between mother and baby by her singing. The mother's body moves with the rhythm of the song and the baby feels this regular pulse as one would feel a massage. Lullabies have swinging rhythms with a '1-2' beat. This swinging beat is also associated with sea songs, rocking ships and the swell of the sea.

Low pitch is felt more strongly in the body than high pitch, hence lullabies are naturally sung at a low pitch in every language and culture. The mother, or mother figure, singing to the baby goes back further in evolution. Many mothers in the animal kingdom do the same. It is the primary comforter, soother, and encouragement to calm and sleep.

Everyone appears to respond to the sound of this low 'mother voice'. It is considered 'sexier', which of course it is, because it reflects the area associated with sex. This voice contributes to courtship, mating and reproducing our unique species. Certainly if you look at female musical roles in Opera and Music Theatre, the woman with the low voice is generally the sexually mature character, whereas the virginal girl with the high moral tone usually has a high voice. A low voice makes a woman more desirable. The high 'twittery' speaking voice is also associated with being socially and intellectually immature

So the women with the full, resonant voices who sing and talk to their unborn child provide the role model, in both boys and girls, for full vocal development of the next generation. The child with this advantage gains a free and natural musical instrument to play, controlled by the ear. This early connection between ear and voice also assists the learning of speech and later, the learning of a second and third language. If father and the rest of the family (close and extended) support and encourage singing in the child *by doing it themselves*, the child will easily and naturally acquire the developed skills of language, singing and communication, as part of normal family activity.

Where there is no natural mother to be the role model, the mother figure can fulfill this role by making a vocal bond with the baby as soon after the birth as possible. Grandma, aunt, nurse, can all do it.

Nature has shown us the best way and without it we will have to make up for that in whatever way is possible. In the absence of any primary vocal link with a mother, or mother figure, the child may have to acquire most of its language skills through learning to read text. Text, which can only develop the eye/voice relationship, should only be a *support* for ear/language development. It should not lead the process of learning language. Text is not language, as you will discover in Chapter 10 - *Words and Rhythm*.

The development of each present day human can be seen as an overview of the process of evolution. In the embryo stage our respiratory and vocal systems resemble the gills of a fish. The respiratory and vocal tract forms from these gills, called branchial arches, during the foetal stage. We are born a helpless creature unable to fend for ourselves. Between birth and approximately 14 months the infant passes through a series of developmental stages, or reflex patterns, which form a sequence. They correspond with the development of the upright biped – the human – in evolution. The following table shows the corresponding stages.

Rolling	Amphibian
Pushing up off the floor	Reptilian
Crawling on all fours	Four-footed
Standing upright	Upright Biped

This sequence of early reflexes enables the helpless infant to become an upright 'staggerer' on two feet in about 12 months.

These stages are all part of the process that produced the upright biped we call Homo Sapiens – the human being, which had all the potential for organization and communication skills. Language then developed for another 95,000 years before the development of writing occurred, only 5,000 years ago. The important message is that the ear/voice relationship, language and communication skills needed all that time to develop before the eye introduced another set of problems. Likewise, the child needs to develop a stable relationship between listening and vocalizing/language skills before the eye relates the spoken word to the written word.

Up, up, up and away

If we accept the evolutionary story and its relationship with our own personal development, then reading and writing skills need to be a tool to *aid and support* development of language and communication skills and not a tool to drive it. The child needs to acquire an extensive 'prattling' language and the confidence to voice thoughts and experience from his or her own fantastic world. The 'too early too much', fantasy of visual images currently available to children could overwhelm the delicate development of personal imagination and the means to express it. Communication is not merely the selection of the correct words. The child needs to listen to inner, earlier experiences of sound, and then imagine *how* to utter the chosen images. It is the use of imagination to colour the voice with resonance and pitch that makes the difference.

Because the infant is so helpless in the early stages of life, and yet has such an enormous capacity to respond to outside stimuli, it is very easy for well meaning parents to introduce the next stage of development before the child has worked out and assimilated the one it is learning now.

If the infant constantly struggles to raise the head and push itself up, resist sitting the baby in a baby carrier to enable it to see around: the baby needs to struggle and work to lengthen and strengthen the spine. If the child climbs up on furniture without first crawling, do not see it as a 'forward child' and buy a baby walker so that it can achieve what it is struggling for - walking? Crawling is an essential stage in the strengthening of the back. Every stage of development needs to include some personal struggle to make a child strong. A long period of crawling is making sure that when the child stands it has the strength in the back to do so.

Early development of intelligence

The importance of music in the development of primary intelligence is already recognised. You are encouraged to play Mozart and other classical music to your baby, both before and after it is born. Apparently a baby is more likely to go to sleep to a classical CD, and the music will also subliminally influence intelligence.

The voice is the only musical instrument that reflects every moment of your life, every thought. All other instruments are safely tucked up in their cases while the rigours of life are played out. When you sing to someone they receive a little of *you* directly - a sound created by living tissue. This has more effect than the best symphony orchestra, band, quartet, or any other instrumental group, however excellent. A professional voice will never have the effect of the voice of someone you love singing, talking or playing to you - warts and all. Professionalism must, by definition, build distance and objectivity into skill. Nothing can replace the mother, or mother figure, singing to her baby.

Periods of quiet are just as important as periods of listening. Silence is a very good listening tool. The world is so full of noises that fragment the most concentrated thoughts of a mature mind. The infant is collecting a repertoire of sounds and learning to refer those sounds back to their source. It cannot cope with too many sounds at a time. Careful listening and concentration begins at this age with the repetition of familiar voices and natural noises against a background free of a constantly running television, radio or music player, even if it is playing Mozart.

While the infant is learning to stand, and listening and responding to the surrounding world of sound, important mechanical changes are also occurring in the voice mechanism itself.

Breast Feeding and infant tongue position

We are born with the tongue entirely in the mouth, the lips having a 'rooting reflex', which grabs and clings. The tongue milks the nipple against the back of the hard palate.

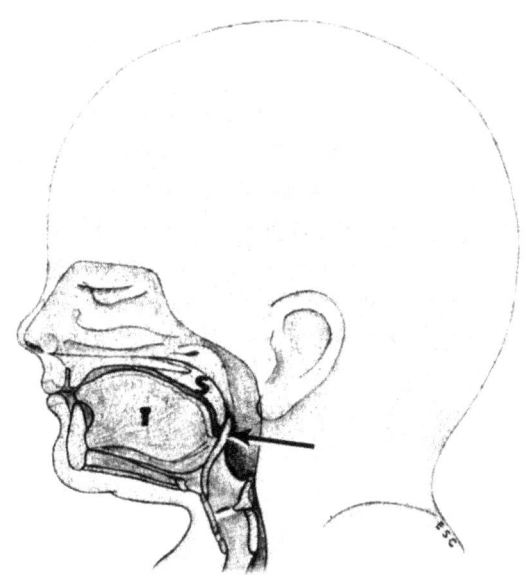

Infant tongue and larynx position (reproduced from Crelin, 1987)

The arrow shows the soft palate (S) locked into the epiglottis during feeding.

The larynx needs to be high in the throat so that the soft palate – the soft extension of the hard palate – can lock into the epiglottis. This prevents the breast milk from entering the larynx during feeding, even though the larynx is suspended in the gut. With this locking device the baby can suck and breathe at the same time. For safety the baby is unable to breathe through the mouth at all: the mouth is exclusively for feeding. This is why the baby is so distressed when the nose is blocked through a cold. Only by loud screaming will the larynx be pulled down the throat to allow air in through the mouth. This early obligate nose breathing establishes nose breathing as the fundamental breathing system and it should remain so for life. During the first 6 months, solid food is introduced, the baby listens and looks around more and the posture of head and neck begins to change. The neck gets longer and the mouth loses its pert, rosebud shape in favour of a wider smile and a broader hard palate. The tongue is no longer needed exclusively for feeding and begins to change its position in the mouth. The tongue is attached to the hyoid bone and larynx and gradually the whole breathing/voice complex begins to shift down the throat. This shift begins about 6 months old when suckling is losing its importance because other food is introduced. However no major tongue shift occurs until the baby pushes itself up on its hands in the first stage of getting upright on two feet.

No other biped has this stage of development because no other biped needs to pull the larynx from its position behind the mouth to a position where it lies roughly at the level of the 7th cervical vertebrae. But this low larynx is necessary for speech. So a baby lying on the floor on its tummy will push itself up on its hands, look around, and make much more noise because that front stretch is pulling the larynx down the throat to the position where speech will be possible.

By the time the baby is climbing up the furniture to stand, gravity is also working on this heavy mechanism with all its weight suspended from the skull. When your young child jigs about and bangs its feet on the floor to music it is shaking its larynx suspension into a position where it can produce the language that is the evolutionary inheritance of Homo Sapiens.

By the time the infant is 2 years old you will be hearing combinations of vowels and consonants that roughly correspond to the building bricks of family language.

The Importance of Rhythm

What is rhythm? How does it develop? How do I make sure my children can respond to rhythm?

At birth a baby has no control over voluntary movement. The baby responds to environmental stimuli through the primitive reflexes, which are autonomic stereotyped responses. As the infant begins to grow and mature through the first six months of life, so the Central Nervous System also begins to mature. Early survival patterns are inhibited to allow for more mature response patterns, or postural reflexes. These allow the child to make the movements that stimulate and strengthen the postural muscle system. As we all develop the same paired postural muscle system and inherit the same early reflex patterns, you can see all growing babies go through the same movements to achieve standing and walking. The foot contact with the floor suddenly becomes a big thing in a child's life. Hearing any rhythmic pattern will initiate an immediate response to bob up and down or bang the feet on the floor in the 'one – two', 'left – right' action of walking. This is not necessarily the next great dancer. This child is stabilizing walking and other more complicated movements by introducing rhythm into the whole postural system. From now on every activity can be learned in relation to this basic rhythm of walking. We refer to a good integration of rhythm and movement as 'well co-ordinated'.

Internal rhythms

So far rhythm has been considered only in response to some outside source. What about the internal rhythms that keep us alive, such as the breathing system, the heart and circulation of the blood, the nervous system, action and reaction of muscles, swallowing, the rhythm of peristalsis that moves the food we eat through the digestive tract? By co-ordination we mean integration of:

- Rhythm of movement, generated by voluntary muscle
- Internal rhythms, generated by involuntary smooth muscle or autonomic systems
- External rhythm we want to connect with and apply to a task

Take a moment to consider what an amazing creature we are; that we throw a ball, drive a car, open a door and walk through it as we hold a conversation. We take these tasks for granted once we have learned them and all this is precise co-ordination of internal rhythms and movement directed by an outside source.

There is another important internal rhythm fundamental to balance and co-ordination.

The Cranio Sacral Rhythm

The spaces between the different sections of the brain are filled with a fluid that totally encloses and cushions the brain, then flows down the spinal canal to encase the whole of the central nervous system. It forms the cooling system for the electrical circuit we call our brain and central nervous system. As in all cooling systems, the coolant must move and moving it involves a pump action. The pump action is rhythmic. The fluid is called the cerebrospinal fluid (brain and spine)

The rhythmic pattern of flow is called the cranio sacral rhythm because it flows between the cranium and the sacrum of the pelvis.

The bones of the skull move as an interactive pump to move this fluid at a rate of about six cycles per minute and the rhythm of the pump results in skeletal shifts through the structures of spine and cranium.

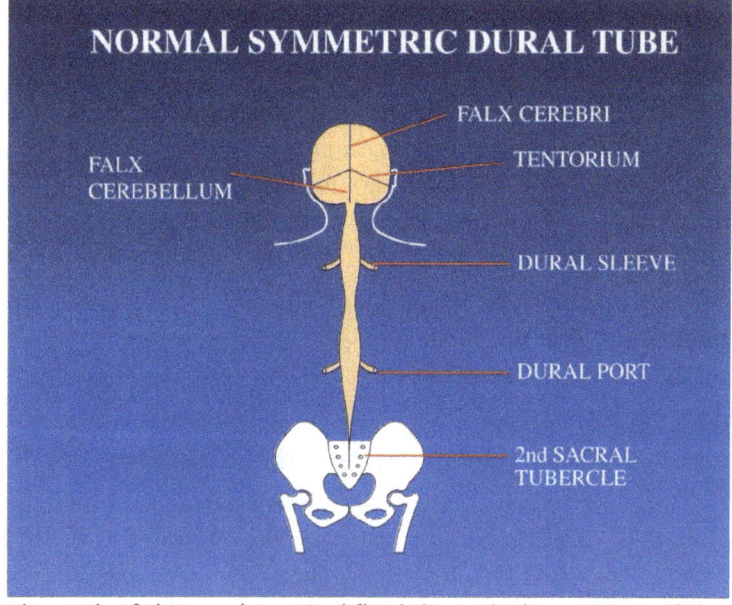

The path of the cerebrospinal fluid through the sections of the brain and along the spinal cord (reproduced from Howat, 1999)

The pumping of the cerebrospinal fluid around the brain and central nervous system is a fundamental body rhythm, which depends for its efficiency on the symmetry of the paired bones of the cranium. The bones of the cranium never completely fuse together. There is always movement between the bones to pump the cerebrospinal fluid. The clinical disciplines of cranial chiropractic and cranial osteopathy check and maintain the efficiency of this rhythm.

We can lose our sense of rhythm at birth

The struggle of the infant down the birth canal is nature's way of kick starting many of the rhythms in the body, including breathing and the cranial sacral rhythm. The bones of the skull suffer major compression during birth but nature has compensated for this by determining that a baby's skull should remain soft and pliable through the birth process so that the bones can be squeezed together without permanent damage. In the weeks immediately after birth the skull recovers from this compression as the rhythms of breathing, sucking and cerebrospinal fluid grow stronger and stimulate each other. These rhythms may be inhibited by:

- a difficult birth with a long labour,
- a very fast delivery,
- a Caesarean Section,
- induced labour,
- a forceps delivery,
- a vacuum delivery.

Closer scrutiny of the position and function of the two temporal bones, which can be viewed paired in the diagram of skull extension, shows the importance of symmetry. Those paired bones each individually house one half of several important body systems requiring symmetrical pairing for efficiency. The temporal bones house:

- the ear and the paired hearing mechanism,
- the paired balance mechanism,
- the paired styloid processes that suspend the breathing system, the tongue and the voice mechanism,
- the paired joints between skull and jaw – the temporo-mandibular joint.

If the temporal bones become asymmetrical during the birth process, and the systems housed in the temporal bone lose their pairing through the birth traumas described earlier, evolution's system of recovery may be stretched beyond its possibilities. In the long term, asymmetrical movement of the temporal bones may adversely affect breathing, singing, speaking, dental development and postural integrity in the developing child. If this problem not corrected, it could affect performance in all those activities that depend on efficient breathing, listening, balance and communication throughout life.

Easy prevention

Either a cranial osteopath or a cranial chiropractor can check babies for cranial symmetry during the early weeks when nature is working to correct compression during birth. The cranial rhythm is the 'mother' rhythm of the body. When this is well established in the developing child all other rhythms; breathing, sleeping, swallowing, crawling, walking, climbing, running swimming, and speech develop with so much more stability.

The sophisticated rhythm patterns of multi-directional sport, or playing music can be acquired with enjoyable ease on this stable rhythmic and co-ordinated foundation (for more information see the useful contacts section at the end of this book).

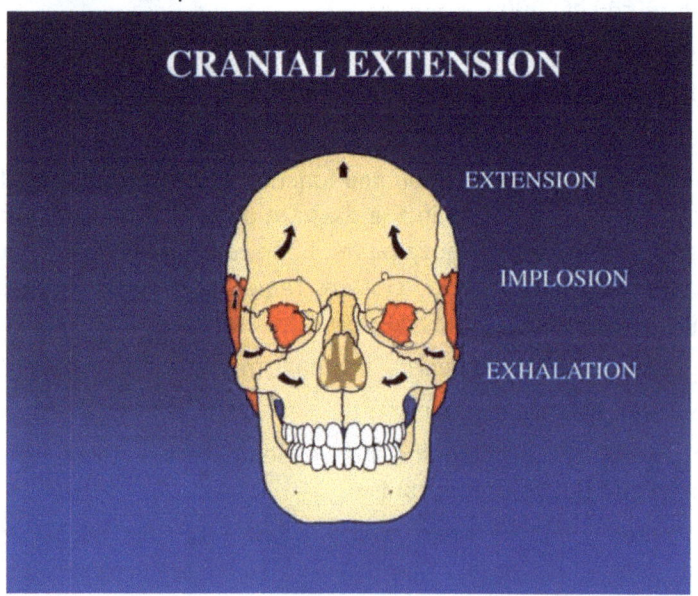

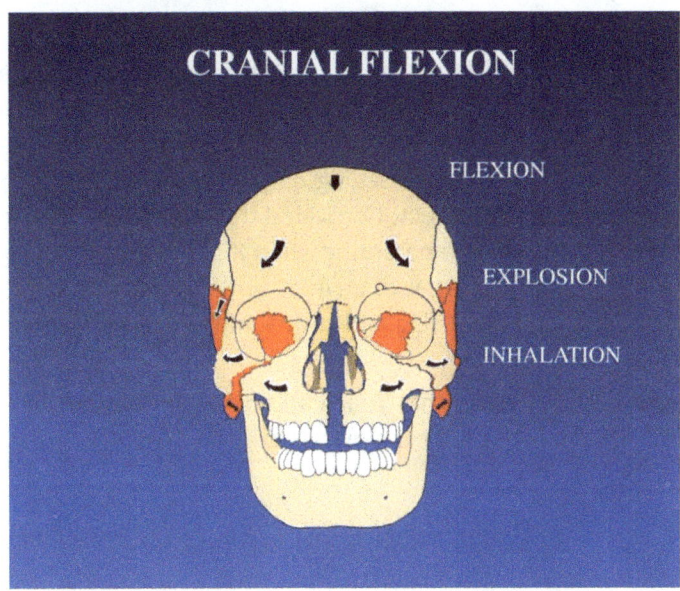

Movement of the cranial bones pumps the cerebro-spinal fluid: extension is a narrowing movement, flexion is a widening movement (reproduced from Howat, 1999)

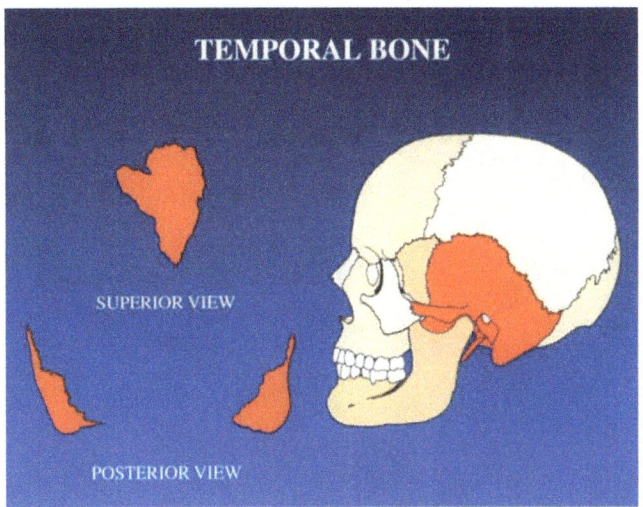

The Styloid Process, the vocal/breathing suspension, the TMJ and the ear hole are all housed in the Temporal Bone: this bone is mentioned in most chapters of this book (reproduced from Howat, 1999)

The End of the Beginning

We have come such a little way in years and months, but the influence that almost daily infant development has on long-term vocal, athletic and musical skill is difficult to appreciate. Here is this little creature, helpless in worldly terms, and apparently needing only a secure, warm and well fed existence. Certainly if they are not provided the infant will make it known. It is easy to feel satisfied with parenting when those conditions are met, but ability begins here if the voice is to develop both speech and singing, if this child is to make music, run, skip and turn somersaults with confidence at some stage of adult life.

You may already realize that *your* early development left much to be desired, but what about the next generation?

3. Early Development - Childhood

The toddling stage

Speech and recognisable tunes formalise as upright posture is achieved. Upright toddlers bang their feet on the ground and rhythmically develop monosyllabic names for things and people. The police car and the ambulance become Bah-bah-bah-bah. Familiar faces become Ma-ma, Da-da, Na-na, etc. The favourite real word is usually 'NO!' This is easy for the toddler to say, taking into account the position of the tongue and the mechanical possibilities at this age. 'Yes' is mechanically just about impossible. The word for 'Yes' in Finnish is 'Ma' I wonder if small children in Finland are more likely to be obedient?

Of course the child will only speak and sing if speaking and singing are all around. Natural voices issuing from all the people who can be reached out to and touched give both encouragement and permission: adults, children, strangers, parents and friends: The face, head and neck muscles are exercised by listening to stories and word games in different languages and dialects on familiar voices. Poetry, songs and nursery rhymes are most easily copied because they are rhythmic and fun. The child loves everything that is rhythmic and fun

Crawling is vital for back strengthening and co-ordination

The stages of rolling and crawling develop the cross patterns in arms and legs we use to walk. All children need to crawl to learn this cross patterning, but not all children do. Bottom shufflers and those who stand without this stage of development need to be checked by the osteopath or chiropractor. They are likely to be suffering an asymmetry in the skeletal structure, resulting in the pelvis being lifted on one side, which will certainly inhibit good voice development, if not all other activities requiring good co-ordination.

The toddler experiments with balancing and this selects specific muscle patterns for control of upright posture in standing, sitting, movement, etc. The self-righting mechanisms of the body are stimulated by 'on the edge' balancing and all children love activities, which make you do this. Given the choice between safe and risky the child will choose risky because there is a natural desire to stretch physical ability. First teeth are appearing during this period of change from infant to toddler in a palate already rhythmically massaged into continuous widening by the tongue and by developing speech and singing. The upright trunk in sitting; reaching with arms for climbing possibilities; rotation of head on neck to find the next place to cling, all provide a gravitational stimulus which causes the following changes in the breathing and vocal mechanism:

- The larynx shifts further down the throat to the adult position, where it will remain for the rest of life.
- The lower position increases the airway and encourages a much deeper 'in-breath'.
- The possibility of a greater in-breath provides the possibility for increased physical activity,
- Increased physical activity works abdominal muscles and all the throat and sinus spaces harder
- More activity in the throat spaces and sinuses promotes healthy ears and a healthy 'middle ear', in which 'glue ear' is less likely to strike.

The vocal suspension is now fully flexible. Singing, skipping and other physical activities enjoyed between 2 years old and 6 years old increase the down spring in the larynx and the rhythm in speech. This makes reading and talking easier and more enjoyable to do.

The increased down spring shifts the tongue to its final position with two thirds in the pharynx. Only one third now remains in the mouth. The main strength of the tongue now articulates in the back of the mouth, which helps develop the *back* of the hard palate, making room for the molar teeth.

As the breathing and voice mechanism gradually shifts lower, speech and singing can become more and more efficient due to the changing position of the tongue (see Chapter 6 - *The importance of Tongue Position*).

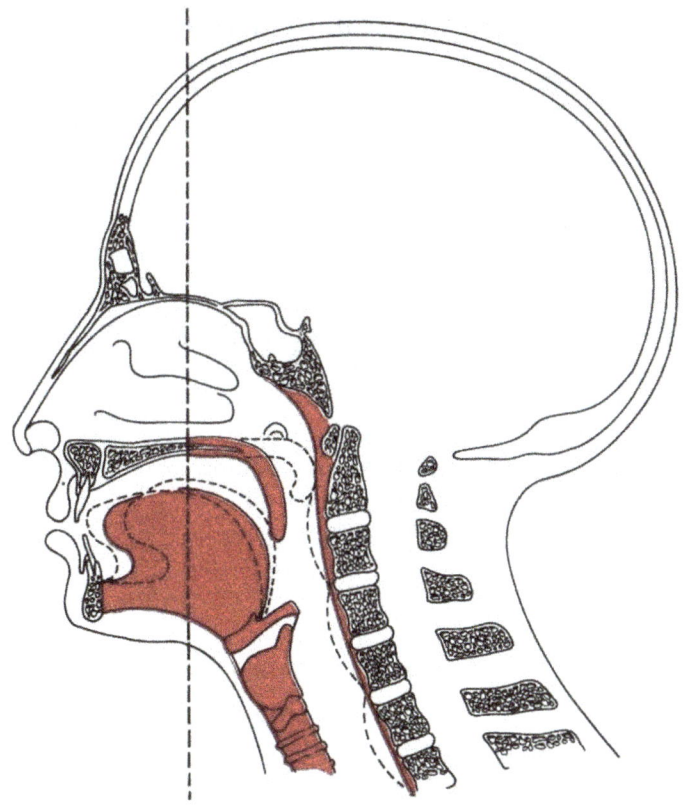

Tongue position at two years old: the tongue and larynx have moved back and down from the infant position

This is the time to make sure that thumb or finger sucking does not become a habit. An active child is less likely to have time to put a thumb into the mouth but of course children are not active all the time and there is usually a favourite bit of blanket or other material as a comforter. A gentle discouragement is needed and a little ingenuity so that the tongue is not pulled back into the mouth by the action of sucking, but allowed to continue its natural movement backwards and downwards. Thumb sucking will interfere with the good development of the face and may displace early teeth in the dental arch. The combined thrust of thumb and tongue can drive the roof of the mouth up instead of allowing the natural broad development that ensures sufficient room for all the adult teeth (see Chapter 9 - *Jaws and Teeth*).

Six years old is a Crucial Stage in Human Development

Voice and the breathing system
- The period of shift for the larynx and tongue is completed by the age of six years (Crelin, 1987)

Dentition and the jaw/skull relationship
- Deciduous dentition begins at approximately nine months and changes to mixed dentition at approximately six years (Hiatt and Gartner, 1987)
- By age six, about 90% of head growth and 80% of jaw growth has already occurred (Van de Linden et al. 1986)

Lateral thinking
- Goddard (2002) suggests that there is a moment in the learning-to-read process at which the balance in the brain tips from right to left, and that this is at approximately 6 - 7 years of age. Lateral and organised thinking is now possible.

Posture
- Upright, balanced and co-ordinated posture and its controlling central nervous system (CNS) matures between 6 and 8 years (Goddard, 2002).

It is reasonable to assume that this is not coincidental, but that development of the child's CNS, voice, posture and deciduous dentition are interdependent.

Childhood

Because of this maturity, the period between 6 and roughly 11 can be an exciting period of discovery. Now is the time to acquire sophisticated language because the equipment for articulation is competent. This is the best age to acquire a love of poetry, before 'left brain learning' dominates school schedules. It is also the age to discover music through playing it, before a fear of not getting it right invades curiosity and learning through play.

It is important to learn to read music as early as possible, so that it becomes second nature to read both horizontally and vertically. When, later, you want to sing to a backing track, you need to be able to follow what is happening in the accompaniment as well as reading your own words to sing the tune. Children of this age are easily stimulated. Given the time and attention from a caring adult, playing an instrument and singing is as interesting as anything else, but you need someone to do it with.

The recorder and the voice are ideal instruments to begin with because neither involves holding a heavy instrument nor unnaturally pressurizing the breathing system. If the recorder is not taught in school, buy a tutor and a couple of recorders and learn it together.

An even better way would be to buy a small keyboard, one that stands on a table, and learn to play chords to accompany the singing and the recorder. This is very easy and great fun. In a short time you will have also begun to sing and accompany yourself. This is the beginning of family music and once it steps across a generation it is likely that your children will carry on that tradition.

There is no need for music lessons until the music making gathers enough momentum for the child to outgrow your efforts and encouragement. By that time physical development should be able to cope with a bigger instrument that may need to be held in front.

The voice is not generally referred to as a musical instrument. We 'play' the piano, the clarinet, the guitar and we 'sing'. The voice is the fundamental musical instrument from which all others sprang and it is important to note that whatever instrument you play, you still need to sing the music you are playing in your head. Beethoven wrote whole symphonies when he was deaf from the power of the music in his head. This inner ear develops from singing, hearing it in others and doing it yourself when you are young.

Children who sing out of tune

These childhood years are often the time when singing is thoughtlessly taken out of your life. You do not grow and mature in a symmetrical pattern, especially during the ages 6-11. Children can be long and lanky one year, muscular and athletic the next. Teeth fall out, physical strength comes and goes, and ability swings between capable and 'can't do a thing'. One day the child is brimming with confidence, the next the child is afraid of failure. All this is typical of a perfectly natural growth pattern.

Take any singing class, any week of any of these years and give them a song with a moderate pitch range. Most of the class will sing it easily There will be some children, however, who struggle with this particular pitch because breathing, voice, muscles and bones are presently changing their relationship and are uncoordinated today. These children may sing out of tune; some may cover this by being disruptive and may not be selected for special music activity. There will also be a few who do not open their mouths at all because they know there is no way they can utter anything that is acceptable.

50 years later these people seek a singing teacher to help them to overcome the fear and horror they experience every Christmas, every birthday party, or any celebration where this dreaded noise will escape. If children had their singing class in the school hall where they could skip and run and move in time to the music, bodies and voices would maintain a better degree of coordination throughout these years. Rounds, songs and singing games should be taught from voices, not from pianos.

Case History

Audrey began singing lessons at the Centre seven years after the death of her husband. She had not been able to grieve for him. There was no way to express what she felt. She frequently wept but it did not connect with the deep sorrow she felt. She had never had the opportunity to sing, could not do it, and didn't know where it was in her. She had been born in, then, Southern Rhodesia in a colonial family and 'one simply did not sing'. She came for lessons and accessed more and more of her voice. She had fun with VoiceGym and looked forward to attempting her first song. She began to sing 'Send in the Clowns' badly out of tune at first, but it was there that her well of grief began to empty. As she sang the song, out of tune, she wept. Something in the words connected and her voice was now resonating inside her. We referred to it as 'leaking', put a toilet roll on top of he piano and she continued to alternately sing and weep. With time the leaking was all done and Audrey began to develop her singing. She is now in a choir that meets on Thursday evenings to sing folk music from all over the world in various languages, all in parts. She loves it. She sings in tune and she has moved on from her grief.

> Piping down the valleys wild ,
> Piping songs of pleasant glee
> On a cloud I saw a child
> And he laughing said to me
> "Pipe a song about a lamb"
> So I piped with merry cheer"
> "Piper, pipe that song agaim"
> So I piped
> He wept to hear.
> "Drop thy pipe, thy happy pipe;
> sing thy songs of happy cheer"
> So I sang the same again,
> While he wept to hear.
> "Piper, sit thee down and write
> In a book that all may read"
> So he vanished from my sight
> And I plucked a hollow read
> And I made a rural pen
> And I stained the water clear
> And I wrote my happy songs
> Every child may joy to hear.
> (William Blake)

All children must be encouraged to sing, run, skip and balance a little every day to gain postural awareness and efficient development of the upper respiratory tract. Runny noses, asthma, middle ear infection and uncontrollable hyperactivity currently appear to be on the increase. Can it be related to the decline of this kind of play? Parents must be made aware that good posture, efficient breathing, and a confident voice are not being developed in our society. Important developmental 'windows' are not being opened in early childhood. Singing, climbing, balancing somersaulting and tumbling stimulate bone growth, efficient breathing, co-ordination, reading and intelligence. Learning through play, and voicing what you have learned, is the quality learning and that is the foundation of a wonderful voice. Your particular childhood gives it to you - or not.

All the old street games, which involved voice - and for good reasons - have been replaced by the voiceless computer game at the cost of voice, posture and co-ordination

Children need to get off the computer and back into the playground and parents need to take them there and join in

4. The Adult Voice

It is so easy to give a totally unhelpful model when describing the voice. There is no adult voice. There is only an adult person whose voice reflects the way they are, think, relate to people and take responsibility for themselves. If the mechanism of the voice is always used naturally and you and your voice develop throughout life in parallel, always voicing your thoughts and feelings, failures and successes, the voice will take on an adult resonance as you take on an adult resonance.

The public speaker or lecturer is often required to interpret and express what others have said or discovered. Much of singing consists of finding personal connections with age-old emotions and experiences. No one can achieve this without first experiencing their *own* adult emotions and thoughts and, most importantly, talking and singing about them to find the connection with personal sensitivity. This is the base from which to explore the art of voicing other people's work, other people's sensitivity. The presenter, actor or singer that cannot relate personal experience to the performance is merely reading or singing the text. People listening can hear that in the voice.

Puberty

All young people want to sing the pop music of the day. It is an industry with huge marketing potential and much of it is directed at youth. It is their music with their energy, expressing their feelings. Like all material untested by time, there is good, bad and horrid. Classical voice training issues a constant tirade on the damage to voices and musical standards caused by the mindless banality of words, tunes and accompaniments (backing tracks). But there is a plus side too.

Many young people write their own music and get together to play it. This has not happened since the death of the folk music culture brought about by urbanization during the industrial revolution. Folk music that survived became the property of the composer and arranger, the academic collector, The Folk Music Society and the classically trained singer. Composers like Britten, Warlock, Quilter and Vaughan Williams turned the folk song into an Art Form for the concert hall. We may yet be spawning a new generation of real folk culture. Originality is often crude in its early struggles against received wisdom.

Young voices are discovering improvisation and chord structures and they are learning through trial and error to build their vocal tuning and resonance on that. This is the way the voice mechanism naturally develops its pitch and tuning (see Chapter 11- *A Voice for Life*), not from a scale progression but from chords that suggest pitch to a free and responsive ear/voice relationship. One only has to hear a classically trained singer attempt to step outside classical musical structures to realise the limitation imposed by that system. New developments from the pop culture may open the way to a new vocal freedom.

The new and younger generation of men want to sing. Robby Williams has done more to encourage young men to sing than the graded, step-by-step, examination syllabuses of the Music Colleges ever achieved. There are currently as many young men working through the *VoiceGym* programme as young women. To someone who has worked with voices for some forty years this is wonderful and new. These young men have not been treble choristers; they have not come from 'musical' families. They are daring to get up for Karaoke, like the gladiator taking up the fight to impress his peer group, and when they have dared and done, they want to do it better. As they get to do it better their musical sights extend and curiosity for other repertoire creates their first problem. This is not a voice problem, but a problem of an educational void. They have no music language with which to learn the new music for themselves.

I have great hopes for the young pop singers. They are fresh and inquisitive and want results. They question established musical standards and are not deceived by jargon. Music needs such people if it is to survive as a living culture.

Moving on

The child's voice changes during the years of puberty to an adult voice. There are no rules here, no stability that allows for a system of vocal development. As with every other facet of puberty, when something stabilizes, you work with it. If it doesn't, you tread water until it does.

What we call 'voice breaking' occurs in both boys and girls. The child's voice lacks a connection with emotion. This does not mean children are not emotional and do not have feelings, just that it is not reflected in the sound of the voice. Thus a child will say, "I love ice cream" or "my rabbit died", with exactly the same voice. One accompanied by a smile, the other tears.

Changes from child to adult

- The frame suspending the voice mechanism (your whole skeletal structure) becomes bigger. The larynx then travels even further down the throat on the in breath creating an even bigger down spring (see Chapter 6 - *The Importance of Tongue Position*).
- Increased use of language exercises tongue, soft palate and translation of the jaw
- A greater range of physical activity exercises breathing systems and strengthens the back.

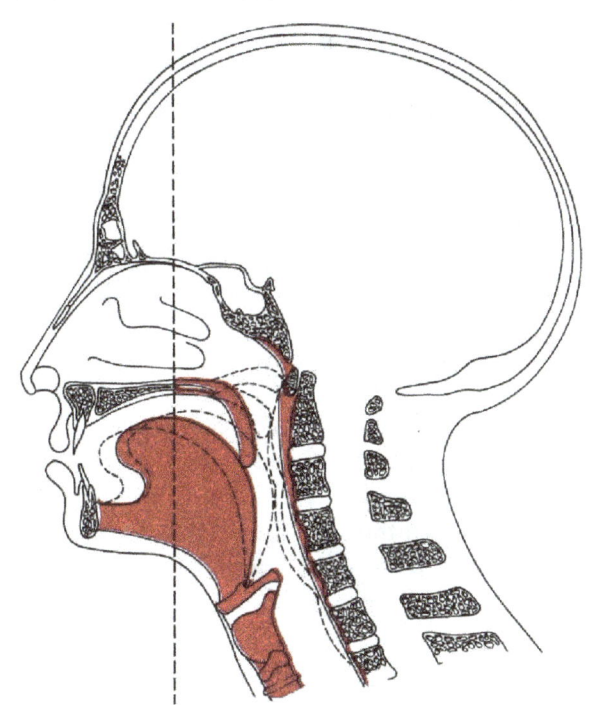

Adult Tongue Position

The tongue is now almost entirely behind the dotted line and the larynx is even lower.

The dotted lines show new articulation possibilities.

Hormones are secreted in puberty that increase sexual awareness. Tactile tissue; the red part of the lips, inside of the mouth, the lining of the throat, lining of the vagina and penis, will swell in response to sexual awareness and activity. The hormone rich blood supply that erects the penis in the male and the vulva in the female also erects the vocal folds. The vocal mechanism can now be excited from within in response to emotion and sexual activity, as well as in response to breath and muscle. A huge range of colour and resonance now becomes available and the voice becomes a sexually powerful and emotional force to be reckoned with.

This change is huge, occurs early in the 'teens' and has to be dealt with. Everything you say can suddenly feel and sound different. Next day it may be different again. When you are with someone in your peer group whom you fancy your voice feels thick and unwieldy. You can't get words out. Just a short time ago you would have been teasing, bullying and now none of that works. If that were not unnerving enough, all around you may be talk of what you are going to do with the exam choices for O level. You are conscious of your body, your sexuality, and awkward social behaviour. Your voice doesn't do anything you expect. Most people recognise this state in boys. Boy's voices noticeably drop in pitch and often sound loud and 'upfront'. Boys are generally forgiven a greater degree of rebellion and this aggressive voice sounds part of that rebellion. Far from it, this voice is expressing fear, lack of confidence and a real need for help.

It is not generally known that girl's voices undergo the same change. They either become husky and ineffectual, or very course and loud. Neither is much good to you at the time so the girl may either retreat shyly into her peer group or becomes surly and aggressive.

The Mother Voice

During puberty girl's voices should undergo the change from a shrill, high treble to the naturally low-pitched speech of the woman. It is part of the maturing of the whole female system and linked with the hormonal changes that produce the monthly ovulation cycle. The hormonal changes enlarge the larynx, which then sits lower in the throat. The vocal folds inside the larynx begin to receive the special blood supply carried to all adult tactile tissue, thus making connection between the voice and sexual activity, the voice and emotion, the voice and the rush of adrenalin (feeling of excitement). The girl begins to feel a physical connection between the voice and the muscles controlling the pelvic floor and the two muscle areas begin to interact. This interaction between the lower abdominal muscles and the voice adds lower harmonics to the sound of the voice, making the adult voice pitch sound lower in the adult female by the time she is ready to give birth. When Nature is preparing the woman for reproduction of the species, she is also being prepared to communicate with the baby in utero. Homo Sapiens are the only creatures with sophisticated language skills. The pitch sounds the voice makes can all be heard in the animal kingdom, but Homo Sapiens is the only creature capable of articulating both vowels and consonants Speech is the natural inheritance of the upright biped and the mother passes that on.

Current educational policies among English speaking peoples do not account for the maturation of the voice. The term 'Puberty' has been superseded by 'young person' or even 'young adult'. Unfortunately neither of these terms allow for the period of vocal instability between approximately 12 and 16.

Difficult Times

The relationship between breathing and voice changes in puberty. The hormones released into the blood supply to all tactile tissue – the inside of your mouth, the genitals and other emotionally excitable areas also now begin to feed the vocal folds. When the vocal folds are brought together to make sound, they have already received a blood supply that erects them. Less air is now required to bring them together to make sound. The adult needs less to vocalise than the child but rarely receives this information, mostly goes on to over pressurize the voice to speak and sing.

Summary of Changes

- Articulation muscles have to regroup because the larynx is heavier and has dropped.
- Fear, anger, frustration is evident in the voice as they are felt. This is difficult to deal with. The skill is only learned by experience
- This is the age when established orthodontic treatment would have appliances in the mouth. Yet another pressure to deal with (see Chapter 9 – *Jaws and Teeth*)
- The part erection of the vocal muscles by hormone input means the voice requires less breath to talk and sing in the adult. Breathing levels need to adjust.

This transition demands lots of encouragement to talk at home, school and any other communicative place: a bit like having a new bike with twice as many gears as your old one. You need to ride up all the familiar hills, be amazed how easy it is and get a feel for it.

The person in this vocal 'hot seat' will, left to own devices, use this new voice as little as possible, speak in monosyllables and keep it under wraps because it is scary.

This is when drama sessions, open school debates, lots of singing and the patience and understanding of adult voices around are crucial. This voice will make mistakes and often give the wrong message. Connections between intentions, feelings, judgements on the inside and how it is voiced will not always make sense. Better to *practice* expressing yourself in an unreal improvisation in drama class, than make a mess of something that really matters by losing control in a real situation.

There is no way one's singing can remain stable in all this and so many young men lose their singing when they no longer sing treble with a child's voice. If only music and singing did not provide such a 'shop window' for schools and colleges. The choir is there on Speech Day, at Christmas, at Graduation. It is an indication for parents and governors of the excellence of the music department and the existence of extra-curricula education. There must be opportunity for passing an audition and being a member of the choir, but the real measure of success would be that *everyone* leaves school with a mature and resonant speaking voice for life and that everyone can still sing with enjoyment at the end of schooling. It would be so easy to achieve and not break the school budget.

Girls who are academic high-flyers

The girl with academic flair needs to keep her head down and work. She is likely to spend more time sitting and working to maintain academic standards than most of her peer group. Answers must be correct, and carefully thought through. The brain needs to maintain control of the voice if the voice is always to act appropriately. There is little time or opportunity for experimenting with the voice.

Many girls halt any further development by maintaining control and the result in many female bank managers, lawyers, doctors or teachers is an overdeveloped child's voice that has never been given the chance to mature. Moderate hyperventilation creeps into the breathing system because by trial and error it is discovered to be a way of maintaining vocal stability and 'raising your voice'. Over pressure disconnects the voice from emotion and sexuality, but the most damaging result is the lack of authority in the voice, in just those professions where authority is needed.

Has your voice matured?

Do your recognise your self in any of these situations?

- Problems with being out of breath when speaking or singing. The breathing/voice relationship required for the adult voice has not adjusted. The voice is over-pressurized and you may be moderately hyperventilating.
- Difficulty with singing and moving, walking and talking, losing your voice when tired. Voice and body may not be as well connected as voice and brain.
- Difficulty with speaking other languages, dialects and accents, with imitating giants, witches ghosts and with general imaginative voice play. The more direct control you have of the voice, the less it can play.
- Difficulty with presenting on the 'fly'. Do you need notes or prompt screens to give a talk on your specialist subject? Voice, body and brain are just not connected.
- Are you a woman with a thin, reedy soprano voice who experiences dramatic shifts in the throat when you want to sing something lower and possibly more dramatic? It is often referred to as a 'register break'. See Chapter 11 – *A Voice for Life*, to find out more about this. The whole system is over pressurized and the suspension rigid. The adult breathing/voice relationship has not been discovered.
- Are you a tenor with a thin, reedy voice who has sung as a treble in a church or cathedral choir? These child voices are trained for uniform, pure but penetrating sound and when you train at the level of commitment required for a cathedral choir, you want it to last. A strong enough pressure system can maintain the high child's position of the larynx sometimes to the age of 14 or 15. When nature finally puts her foot down and the voice drops, the adult world of secular music is vastly different. It expresses secular emotions and sexual pleasure. The voice needs other colours, other deeper resonance found only in the pelvis. This voice needs to play, have some musical fun, loosen up and let go. After all – voices are part of us, and we need to play, loosen up and let go.

Disconnection

Speech and singing are in the same instrument, subject to the same functional mechanics but when we go to school these functions of the same voice are generally separated by singing being firmly attached to learning music. Since singing is no longer part of the culture of a modern community (when did you last happen on a group of men or women singing together at the end of their working day?) it has become special to sing. Many people are cut off from singing in the early school years because teachers do not understand how the voice develops and when a child sings out of tune or makes other grim noises it is diagnosed as a poor ear or being unmusical. It is probably just a stage of growth and development where the mechanism is not very well balanced. Come back in six months and the voice would have gone from ugly duckling to swan.

The Ageing Voice

If all stages of voice development are encouraged and there is no 'retirement' of voice, brain and body, the adult voice will continue to fulfil the demand of an ever questioning and curious brain to speak and sing. The results are far reaching. Breathing, rhythms, balancing on two feet, mental alertness, all continue while voice, body and brain excite one another. This part of life is dealt with in detail in Chapter 11 - *A Voice for Life*.

5. Breathing, the Myths and the Mischief

The mandible, tongue, hyoid bone, larynx, trachea and lungs connect in the descending order you see in the model. The trachea (windpipe) splits into two –one branch to each lung. This altogether forms one huge, heavy and mobile suspension. The weight of this suspension is cushioned by the central diaphragm, which divides the breathing and heart mechanisms from all the other body organs.

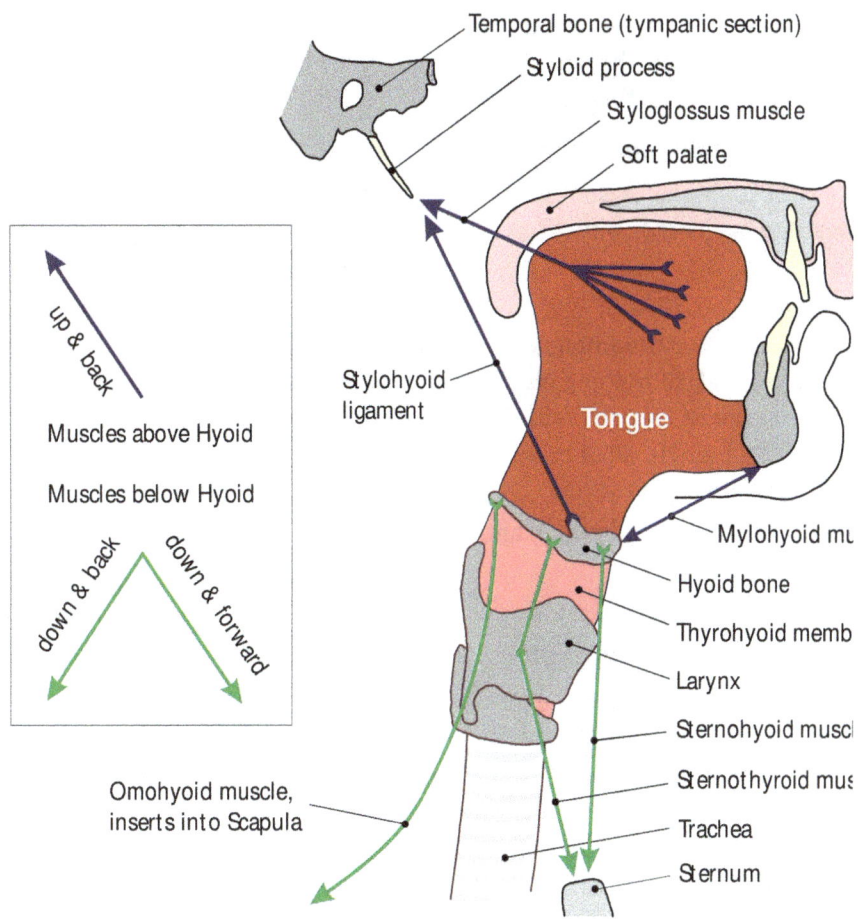

Model of the upper part of the breathing system suspended from the skull

It is impossible to put all of the breathing/voice mechanism into one diagram without making it look like some kind of static pump. Efficiency lies in the very dynamic nature of the entire system and the system connects with every part of us. I suspect that one of the reasons for inefficient use of the voice is the anatomical diagrams we see in books that position everything according to 'dead anatomy'.

Individual parts of the system can be explained precisely, but evolution is economical and uses the minimum number of muscles to execute the maximum number of tasks. The total mechanism of breathing and voice is spread about in all of these chapters. I believe you will gain personal efficiency in your unique system if I give you working models for the specific parts and you put the whole system together for yourself by using all the learning principles this book offers.

The Suspension (opening diagram)

A Suspension is something hanging from a fixed point and having mobility in all other directions. The breathing/voice suspension is designed to:

- Keep you alive. If you suffer a serious fall the suspension takes the shock. Your breathing/voice mechanism bounces and survives intact - you break something else. Time is on your side for someone to fix your collarbone, your fractured skull even, but breaking your breathing system would kill you in three seconds. Evolution wants you alive to reproduce the species.
- Allow breathing, speech and singing in any position the body can move into
- Operate for safety, outside of your direct control.
- Use gravity to reduce effort.

The improvement you experience when reading aloud or singing while bouncing on the ball is partly due to the movement of this great suspension of the breathing/voice mechanism. In many people this suspension is practically rigid.

"Surely if that is how breathing, singing and speaking is designed, the body will develop it naturally. How can I interfere with that? How can it become rigid?"

Hypertension in the suspension

In many different ways people learn to resist gravity in standing, walking, talking or singing by never letting the body come to rest, never letting their body weight totally pass through the body to the floor. More of this in Chapter 8 – *Balance and Posture*.

Too much sitting

Ten years sitting in school, maybe three more sitting in further education and then on and on throughout life sitting and sitting. Balance is lost, forward head, tongue and shoulder posture result once again in hypertension in the suspension.

Find this suspension system for yourself

All of the various muscles and ligaments supporting the breathing and voice system from above are suspended from the Styloid Process on each side of the skull. You have a skull and you can find this on it. Dig your fingers into the depression just behind your ear. About 1cm in from your finger this little bone projects downwards and supports the whole of your breathing system and voice.

It is one of the body's most important junctions. The muscle connections are between the following:

- Styloid process and the tongue - the muscle branches into four as it connects to the tongue (open your mouth and have a look at your tongue and picture this muscle).
- Styloid process and the hyoid bone - span this with finger and thumb.
- Tongue and mandible - poke about under your tongue
- Mandible and hyoid bone - span under your mandible and swallow a few times, speak or sing to feel the movement.

The last two connections form the floor of the mouth (remember this spring from Chapter 1?). A double chin is collapse of one or both of these muscles –a very good reason for learning how to look after the suspension.

Flip back to early development (Chapter 2) and check the information on the Sacral-Cranial Rhythm.

Read about the important role of the temporal bone of the skull in cranial rhythm. The Styloid Process projects from the temporal bone of the skull, which explains why it is so important to align these two bones in infancy. Failure to do so can affect the whole breathing/voice suspension.

On the diagram on Page 44 notice the direction of the pull. It is upwards and backwards. Stand in front of your mirror and put your fingers around the bony larynx suspended in your throat, under your jaw. Move it side to side. Don't worry, it is designed to move, you won't break anything, even though it may feel quite peculiar to do this. Put a finger of the other hand on the dip behind you ear and imagine the muscles suspending the larynx from this point. You can easily detect the backwards and upwards direction of pull.

Total flexibility in breathing and voice

If the suspension of your breathing system were connected only to the skull, suspending it only from above, what would happen when you turned upside down? The breathing system would become seriously displaced up into the back of the nose. This suspension uses gravity to assist operation in whichever position you are in but there are also muscle connections that stabilize the larynx from below between:

- Hyoid bone and sternum - find the two bony 'knobbles' at the base of the neck (this connection is in the space between this secure bony mass and the moveable Hyoid).
- Larynx and sternum - find the moveable larynx again (this connection is slightly shorter than the one before and enables the space to be maintained between Hyoid and larynx).
- Larynx and hyoid - this is a membrane, not a muscle. It ensures that the hyoid does not interfere with laryngeal movement (the larynx merely hangs from the Hyoid).
- Hyoid to shoulder blades, right and left - stand side on to the mirror and look at your upper back (locate your larynx and hyoid. Picture the muscle that could run right and left through a loop at the base of your neck and connect to your shoulder blade each side - one of the most important in the whole suspension).

Hence the breathing/voice mechanism is suspended from both above and below in a double suspension. The double suspension you are most familiar with is probably that in your car (see diagram on next page):

- The upper suspension allows you to go round corners without leaning.

- The lower suspension absorbs the shocks from the road beneath you.

Similarly, the breathing/vocal suspension allows you to breathe and vocalise whichever way up you happen to be. You can:

- Cram yourself, curled up on your back, into a cupboard to fix a water pipe but still breathe and still talk.
- Work in the garden, bending, crouching, and squatting, while talking to your nearest and dearest who is cutting the grass.
- Play on the floor with your children.
- Tie your shoes, or cut and paint your toenails, breathing and talking all the time.

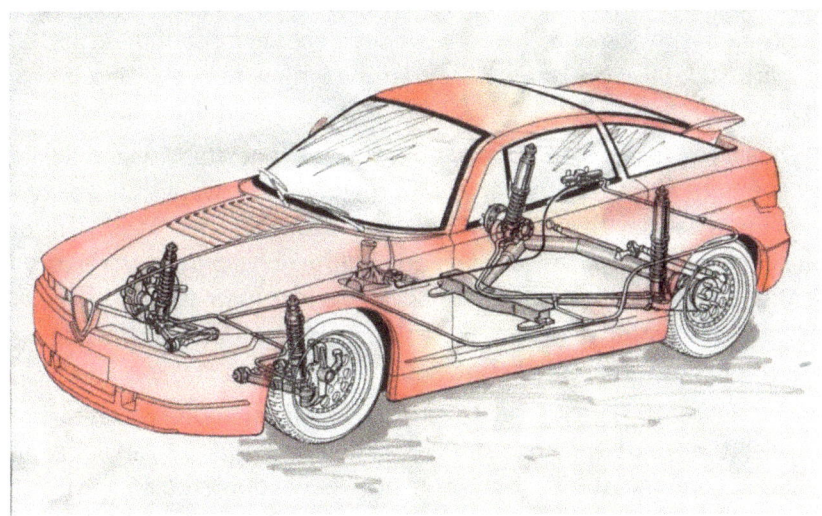

The suspension of your car

The list is endless. On a professional level you can sing operatic roles while hanging upside down from a trapeze, falling downstairs in the mad scene, or lying on your death bed – head lolling over the side. All breathing and vocal challenges can be met if this suspension maintains its 360º integrity throughout life, provided it is strengthened in all these positions.

But we mainly talk and sing in an upright position, thus strengthening only the upper suspension, which suspends the breathing/voice mechanism from the skull:

- Weren't your singing lessons all standing up and singing forward?
- Didn't you sit in school and face the teacher most of the time?
- How many times in your life did you read a poem upside down?

I would be surprised if you have sung Mozart or Puccini, read aloud dramatic poetry, or voiced a passionate and persuasive argument for a rise in salary, while rolling on the floor, sometimes face down. So the upper suspension is strong and may even have pulled the whole mechanism into a slightly higher position than is mechanically desirable, simply because the pull of upper and lower muscles is not balanced.

Many professions are in danger of giving people a permanent slump. Hairdressers, dentists, mothers with small children, teachers, singers and presenters all risk the collapse of neck and back muscles because they mainly deal with demanding people or audiences in front of them and while they are standing, the people they are dealing with are sitting down, or smaller than they are.

The larynx suspension will have the strength and stability and flexibility to cope with all of this forward pull provided that strength, stability and flexibility is developed and maintained throughout the whole suspension. If the people working in forward and down directions in their work, as those mentioned above, were to rebalance the strength in the suspensory mechanism by stretching and exercising in other directions outside work, they would not suffer either damaged backs or strained voices.

If you are 45 and just discovering this information, you had better consider the VoiceGym programme! All is possible - it takes longer and requires more persistence, but I have not yet encountered an age group in which, given the commitment to work at it, posture and voice did not improve.

In 1968 a paper was published that claimed the action of the voice was affected by inefficiency in the muscles which make up the suspension of the larynx, called, in the paper, the extrinsic frame (Zenker and Zenker, 1968). What affects the voice will also obviously affect the breathing system.

I have always found that rebalancing the extrinsic frame by strengthening the upper back with exercise improves:

- Loss of pitch range and tuning

- Loss of seal between the back of the tongue and the soft palate, which is vital in nose breathing and the playing of wind instruments.
- Voice strain due to continuous use. The laryngeal system is designed to work 24 hours a day – we don't stop breathing. Why should the voice, which is using the same system, not be just as efficient and if necessary, continuous?

Now we have located where breathing and voice happen and the connections to the main frame of the skeletal system (e.g. skull, breast bone, shoulder blades).

How does it all work?

Begin by considering the effect of gravity on everything we do. There is no 'up' spring on this planet. There is only 'down' spring and rebound. We punch gravity and use the strength of the rebound to speak or sing. The voice works on 'down' spring.

Experiment

Take a nice sized ball –football size is ideal –bounce and catch it, using both hands to throw and catch and making sure your knees bend with each bounce.

Now say a vowel with each bounce –vowels you say, not vowels your write.

'A' will be as in 'bad', not 'A' as in 'play'

Notice where you sound the vowels in relation to the bounce. For most people the vowel will sound at the bottom of the spring, where the ball gathers rebound. The ball and you will 'sound' together. This is how breathing and voice work within the double suspension.

The diaphragm

The in-breath is initiated reflexly by the vagus nerve activating the diaphragm, which contracts and consequently flattens. This takes support away from underneath the heavy breathing system, resulting in a drop in pressure in the lungs. The whole mechanism suspended from the styloid process, and described at the beginning of this chapter, then falls by its own weight drawing air from the pharynx and sinuses into the low pressure. This whole process is aided by muscles throughout the trunk.

What Should Happen

Step 1. The Diaphragm as a reflex muscle

The diaphragm is reflexly contracted by the Vagus nerve, which fires about every six seconds. Oxygen is an essential food that the body needs in precise amounts to complete the body's efficient chemical balance between oxygen and carbon-dioxide. Antoine-Lavoisier, a Paris Tax inspector, who died on the guillotine in the reign of terror because he overtaxed the city to fund his experiments, discovered the importance of carbon-dioxide in the regulation of oxygen (Henderson, 1940). In forty years of teaching I have never discovered a concern for the balance between carbon-dioxide and oxygen in anyone wanting to sing, but plenty of attempts to take in as much air as possible with every breath and a general belief that the greater the volume achieved in the in-breath, the more 'support' there will be for the voice. Going back to Chapter 4 - *The Adult Voice*, you have already discovered that pressure is not the only agent required to 'fire' the adult voice. As soon as the factor of chemical balance is also considered 'amount' begins to take a back seat and efficiency and the possibility of over breathing (moderate hyperventilation as described by Lum (1975): see *Some medical arguments against cortical control of breathing* on page 54) become more important issues. The simple message is to allow the body to automatically adjust the amount of air required and not reduce your system of breathing to one of cortical control. Exercise for physical efficiency, balance and stretch, learn your functional anatomy and let your reflexly activated diaphragm adjust your breathing to that demand. You are not the best judge of what that demand requires and this includes the sung or spoken phrase.

Necessary Conscious Control

The diaphragm *can* be consciously controlled. We have a 'fight or flight' emergency system for survival. It blasts the system with oxygen, which encourages the body to produce large quantities of adrenalin so that we can hit out in spite of injury, pull ourselves free, or achieve miraculous and extraordinary deeds in the face of personal danger. It is accessed by a sharp intake of breath through the mouth and should only be used in emergencies. You do not want to sing or to give your presentation in a mild state of shock!

Step 2. The Ribs

You have twelve ribs and they are all jointed to the spine. See the diagram on the next page. The floating ribs (the two bottom ribs) are the only ribs with one joint. The other ribs are jointed at the sternum and at the thoracic vertebrae of the spine. There is also a degree of flexibility where cartilage meets bone (see the diagram of the ribs: A. Intercostals from the front). The term 'rib cage' is misleading. The Intercostal muscles can all move *individually*, facilitating individual movement of each rib and fingertip control of lung pressure from the inter-costals. The quality of the ribs as a whole should not be that of a rigid cage, but of a flexible basket, capable of giving under pressure. In addition, the whole basket is capable of rotating and springing back when free to do so, while still maintaining flexibility to individual ribs (see Chapter 8 - *Balance and Posture*)

The recoil of elastic tissue, which has been stretched by the in breath, aids the out breath. This whole spring and recoil system is so elegant in the management of the required volume that one wonders how anyone ever thought that they could manage it better themselves by conscious control.

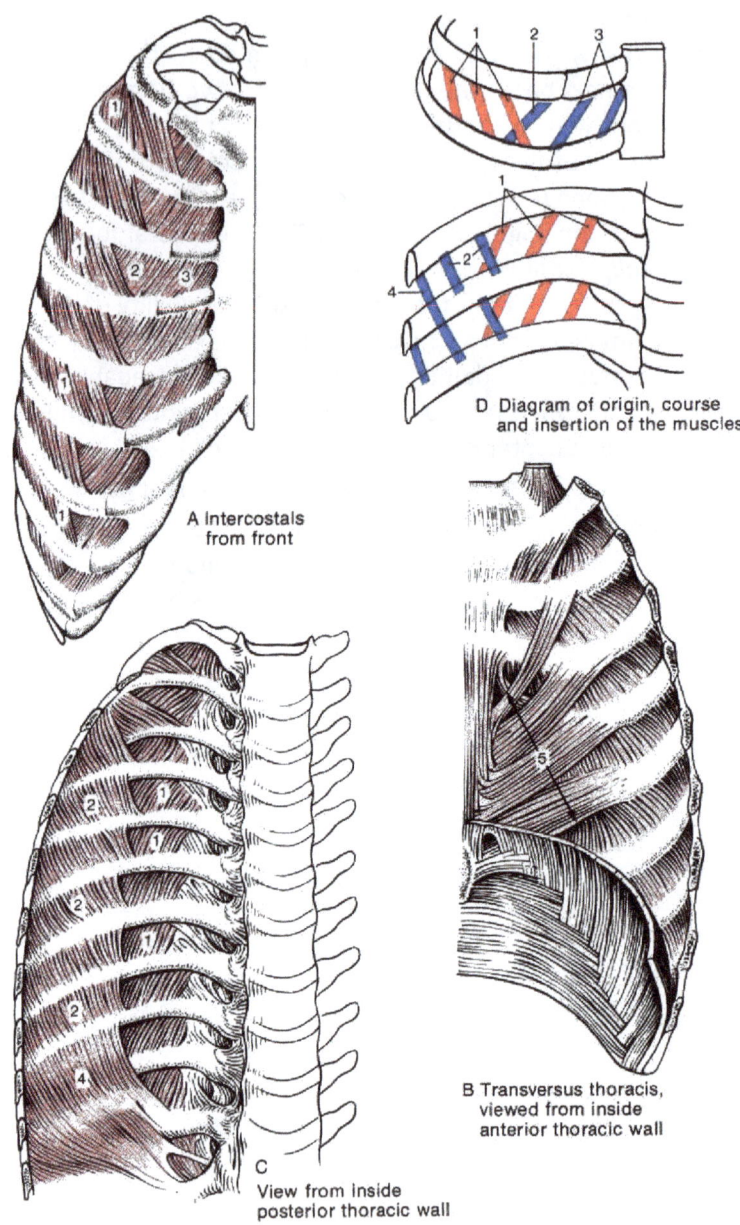

Ribs (Reproduced from Platzer, 1992)

Step 3. Movement of air

Air moves from the Pharynx and nasal sinuses into the lungs where gases can be exchanged and combined to rebalance the body chemistry. Carbon dioxide and nitric oxide are needed to facilitate the combination of oxygen with the haemoglobin of the blood. When air from the nasal sinuses is drawn into the lungs, air is drawn from outside the body into the nasal passages, where it is warmed, sterilized and gathers moisture. Nitric oxide (NO) is produced in the paranasal sinuses and excreted continuously into the nasal airways. Nitric oxide was first detected in the nasal passages in the 1990s and Nobel prizes were awarded to researchers who discovered that the body produced NO (Page, 2003). This is another good reason for breathing through your nose

Amount

This is decided by the balance or imbalance of the body chemistry in relation to demand. So when you swing that axe, imagine the length of that musical phrase or decide to swim the length of the pool, you make a demand for the body to achieve that for you. Henderson (1940) says 'nature provides that in every healthy man or animal, except under intense exertion, the oxygen supply is always ample'. Again: 'Vigorous breathing does not take place *before* an exertion; the exertion is first made and then the oxygen needed to clear the system before the next exertion is absorbed.'

Training the system

First learn and understand the desired task and what it involves. The breathing system must be allowed to develop an understanding of what is required for the task. When you run out of breath do not assume it is because you need more. You may, at that point, need *less*. Co-ordination between gravity, physical balance, exchange of gases, and the suspensory down spring of the larynx may not yet be sufficiently coordinated. Continue to repeat the demand and allow time for the brain, body, and breathing/voice mechanism to organise and then bring it about. Check, for instance, that you are standing equally on two 'hip-joint- width' feet, and when you are singing check that you end the phrase accurately and positively so that the brain knows *when* to breathe.

The muscle systems that form the supporting frame for breathing activity

Pictures of dead anatomy and positions of individual muscles are not any more useful to the breather, speaker, or singer, than is laying out all the bits of the engine for the racing driver. You need understanding of the interaction between the parts and then a good tried and tested working model. Understanding is control. Constantly questioning your information and keeping it up to date protects that understanding.

The muscle system that supports the breathing/voice system will be discussed in Chapter 8 - *Balance and Posture*, as it needs to be understood as a dynamic system of rotation and torque.

Some medical arguments against cortical control of breathing

The function of our respiratory system is not just to push air in and out, but also to maintain a very specific chemical balance. For the cells of the brain, heart, kidneys and other organs to function efficiently our blood requires a concentration of about 6.5% carbon dioxide and only 2% oxygen. At the end of the nineteenth century Russian physiologist Verigo and Dutch scientist Bohr independently discovered that without the presence of carbon dioxide, the oxygen in the blood cannot be used. Oxygen deficiency is therefore not always caused by a lack of oxygen, but can also be caused by a lack of carbon dioxide in the blood (Henderson, 1940: Lum, 1975). When we over breathe we take on more oxygen than we need, causing an imbalance in the amount of oxygen to carbon dioxide in the body. In a mouth breather large amounts of carbon dioxide will be blown out, upsetting the chemical balance still further (Buteyko, 1985).

The following is an extract from "Hyperventilation – the Tip of the Iceberg" a report by L.C.Lum (1975) from Papworth and Addenbrokes Hospitals, Cambridge, England. It is a report on "the fat folder syndrome". This is the large collection of notes on patients who present bizarre and often unrelated symptoms and are passed from department to department by clinicians who can find no solution to the problem. They are finally diagnosed, at the last ditch, as "anxiety state" and sent for counselling. He discovered that the common factor in all of these cases was hyperventilation, not at an instantly recognisable pathological level, but as constant, moderate level of persistent over breathing.

"Symptoms (of hyperventilation) may show up anywhere in any organ, in any system, for we are dealing with a profound biochemical disturbance. Such patients are pursued relentlessly, with every investigative device known to modern science, and end up with the label of 'anxiety state'."

The purpose of breathing is to replenish and rebalance the chemistry – it is not about volume. When the body chemistry is in balance systems work efficiently, including the voice. The diaphragm muscle responds to stimulation of the respiratory centre by changes in body chemistry and contracts to pull in just enough air to rebalance oxygen levels, relative to specific chemical imbalance (Guyton,1977).

Received Wisdom

As well as the teaching of singing, speech and other wind instruments, many different physical exercise disciplines also use controlled breathing as a basic tool of physical control. In-breath and out-breath are often regulated to coordinate with movement, so that the muscular power stroke is always on the out breath. Now there has been so much modern research into the function and chemistry of breathing, musical training and other exercise programmes that train for breathing efficiency may need to rethink their instructions relative to this research.

In the following sections are some examples where rethinking would appear to be necessary

Yoga

Yoga teachers advocate the development of rhythmic and controlled nose breathing as a meditative activity. The silent observation of one's own breathing rhythm induces calm and a tranquil state of mind. Breathing becomes deeper with increased concentration on its flow. But here are some extracts from books on Yoga that introduce yoga as a development of potential.

"Oxygen is the element most used by the body. Senility, poor concentration, and mental fatigue can be caused by lack of oxygen in the brain cells. Deep breathing in the (yoga) poses cleanses the lungs and stimulates the cardiovascular system. Breath is the life force and is directly related to vitality and mental balance" (White and Forrest 1981). This description encourages the view that a greater intake of air provides a greater intake of oxygen and that both are desirable.

Aerobics, Aquacise, Pilates, Step and other Exercise Systems associated with Leisure Centres and Sports Training

Exercise classes always include instructions on breathing. There is a general policy of 'in through the nose, out through the mouth', closing the mouth for the inbreath to prevent mouth breathing and blowing the out breath through rounded lips. "Breathe in to prepare for the movement. Breathe out as you move".

Valsalva Manoeuver.

Breath is associated with power because the technique applied to weight lifting is based on the valsalva manoeuver. By breathing in hard, bracing the mouth and throat and refusing to breath out, the chest forms a pressurised 'brick' which can be used to brace muscles and increase brute strength.

It is easy to pick up this technique and use it to brace yourself in other power-based exercises, where it is not desirable. This could damage your back. Instructions for breathing are often given by people superficially trained in exercise systems (sometimes as little as a weekend) with little backup of functional anatomy.

Instructions like 'empty your lungs fully and relax the ribcage' are common but actually impossible to achieve. There is always a residue of air in the lungs and for safety the ribs are preloaded in favour of breathing in. There is regular emphasis on the need for oxygen (for instance, 'Breath as wide and as full as you can' and 'For the blood to do its work properly it has to be fully charged with oxygen'), the implication being that breathing efficiency is achieved by maximising the in and out motion of the ribs and that the principle regulator is oxygen.

Every teacher knows that in order to get a good response there is often a need to overstate and sometimes border on the inaccurate. However, there does seem to be encouragement to focus on 'amount' here as a fundamental in breathing efficiency and 'amount' is not the efficiency factor, but chemical balance.

The Alexander Technique

The Alexander Technique began with F. M. Alexander's desire to improve his voice. He discovered, by observing the way he spoke and breathed, how much the relationship of head and neck affected the total body behaviour. He then developed a unique system of 'hands on' re-education for unnecessary physical effort. He did not apply his technique to music; there is no record of his doing so, but Alexander Technique is widely used as a relaxation technique by musicians already advanced in the playing of the instrument and finding it stressful. It is taught in all the major UK music colleges and UK colleges specialising in drama training. Alexander applied himself marginally to speech, being more occupied with the direction and inhibition of the head/neck relationship as presented in the occipital joint. He formed a company to perform plays, but it was not successful. The idea of co-ordinated efficiency of simultaneous moving and singing or speaking, as in theatrical performance, was not explored, now were possible connections to other disciplines exploring physical efficiency at the same time, like osteopathy, physiotherapy or chiropractic.

The Whispered 'AH'

The unvoiced whisper, the 'whispered Ah' was developed by Alexander as a tool to correct breathing inefficiency and extend the acquired good postural system. While listening to your own light nose breathing, the out breath is selected to expel air through the mouth in an unvoiced whisper. The whisper is maintained until the autonomic breathing reflex activates the inbreath. At the end of the autonomic inbreath the cycle is repeated. Muscles that have worked hard to expel air while maintaining the constant in the whispered sound achieve a longer resting length, thus pulling in more air with each subsequent inbreath. Efficiency appears to once again be coupled with 'amount' and there is a dangerous tendency to blow off large amounts of carbon dioxide (see *Some medical arguments against cortical control of breathing* on page 54). The whispering encourages vocal folds to not quite approximate, which eventually produces a breathy quality in the voice.

Singing and Speech

There is a general consensus of opinion among writers of books on singing that 'abdominal breathing' where the abdomen is allowed to relax on the in-breath is preferable to 'top rib' or 'clavicular' breathing. In abdominal breathing, the organs within the pelvis are depressed by the descending diaphragm to extend lung capacity. The 'abdominal muscles tighten like a corset to pressurize and expel the air for speech and song' (Bunch, 1993). The *whole* rib basket should be involved in breathing. All the ribs, up to the top ones that lie beside the collar bones, should be exercised for flexibility. The lower ones will naturally expand the lungs more as they are not joined to the sternum but float out as far as exercise and demand has encouraged them to do so. The desire to consciously tighten all the abdominal muscles on the outbreath encourages a bellying out of them on the inbreath. Any bellying out of abdominal muscles on the in-breath is a sign of weakness or lack of understanding of the role of the internal oblique muscles that form the core stability (see Chapter 9 - *Balance and posture*).

There is also agreement that breathing is about amount of air. Phrases like 'greater lung capacity,' 'fill your lungs',' full expansion of your lungs,' 'constant air pressure', 'breath support' all encourage you to expand the cycle of inspiration and expiration with specially directed breathing exercises. All books contain either specific breathing exercises, or at least 'things to do and think' which would change your attitude to breathing in favour of increased volume and direct control.

Oren (1999) stated that 'Breathing exercises are designed to bring reflexive action under cortical control'. There follows ten pages of detailed instructions for exercises to bring this about. I could fill several pages with quotations from books on singing that advocate breathing exercises to increase lung capacity.

Singers following these instructions are in grave danger of developing the valsalva manoeuvre which will pressurize the larynx and drive it up in the throat. In the short term this will improve the ability to sing high, loudly and accurately. Over the long term the voice will become harsh and unlovely, lose its pitch range and finally the singer will have problems of voice loss through extreme sub glottal pressure.

To visit a Music Festival and hear the adjudications for the singing classes is to listen to a continuous tirade against 'lack of breath support', which is apparently responsible for all singing problems; being terrified of singing in public; singing flat; running out of breath; forgetting your words; standing stiffly; standing too relaxed; the list is endless. The message is always the same. Go home and do some breathing exercises to strengthen 'your support'. Could these problems be the 'anxiety states' described by Lum (1975) in his warning about over breathing?

How is it that up to date information on breathing and functional anatomy has not percolated into music teaching?

The mere acceptance of singing and speech as being two separate disciplines as opposed to one – the voice – presupposes that they must behave differently. While singing and speech training remain separate disciplines, accredited by different governing bodies it will always be difficult to gain a concensus on how the voice works. Speech therapy is yet another vocal discipline with no connections to other voice teaching. Speech therapists are not required to sing.

This presents a world of total confusion to anyone wanting to improve their voice. Many people actually believe that their voice needs speech therapy when what it really needs is exercise and understanding. So much information in so many different places; so much information with no central, agreed modus operendus; so many people dealing with just one part of the whole voice-body-brain-system, which needs to breathe for its very existence, not to breathe specially and differently to sing. So many different jargons, philosophies, goldfish bowls, never meeting each other except at conferences, where there are no patients/clients/singers to say "But this did not work for me".

It is too easy in autocratic enclaves, for the Emperor to be without clothes for many years with no outsider to recognise it.

Total vocal flexibility

There is no mention in any of the singing books I have read of a possibility that you may already have an efficient breathing system, gained by some other physical activity. It is apparently assumed that if you want to sing, that is all you have ever considered doing which requires any efficiency of breathing. The layman, coming to singing, finding it a pleasure and wanting to know more about it has the choice of buying a book and reading about it, or could have some singing lessons. I am quite confident that early in the learning curve of either, breathing exercises will be on the agenda. If Tiger Woods went anonymously for singing lessons one wonders whether he would be given breathing exercises as a starter.

I always considered it odd that all my voice training seemed to be done standing two dimensionally still beside the piano. My other love, hockey, which I played most of my life, is a multidirectional sport. The awe generated by the 'Professor of Singing' prevented my pointing out that I never considered my breathing while pounding around the field, but I never ran out of breath, or experienced anything but a feeling that all the energy was arriving where it was needed. I so wanted to ask, "Why do the problems I have with singing increase in relation to the focus I put on controlling my breathing? I didn't ask because I assumed it was failure on my part to understand and do correctly the exercises he was giving me to train my voice.

In just one exercise programme I discovered someone after my own heart. Callan Pinckney (1988) says, in *Callanetics for your Back*, "Breathe normally –don't make it an issue. I do not stress breathing. I have found that if I do, most people start to concentrate on their breathing and begin to tense their bodies".

The Work Song

The abundance of sea shanties, which developed in the days of the tall ships, were not sung by voices that practiced breathing exercises. Or did they? Climbing rigging, hauling on ropes and anchor chains, and working the body fearsomely hard must have developed a pretty efficient breathing system, based on balance and stretch. It certainly produced a heritage of song from hard physical work and lots of stretching. There is much evidence to suggest that it also relieved the monotony, agony and frustration of life at sea.

Sail Training

Picture a tea clipper nosing her way through fog, silent and vulnerable as she edges into harbour, with a seaman astride her bow, calling into the fog or singing a loud shanty, so that other shipping knew the ship was there. Trawlers working together to net the herring communicated ship-to-ship, end of net to other end of net, by voices alone.

The same can be found in the work songs of the common man all over the world. Singing together formed a bond to pull the chain or pick the cotton, but also to express common frustration and anger against working conditions and inhuman practices. The voices expressed gut feelings in ordinary language and were activated by a breathing system built on hard physical work. What of this is left in the 21st Century? Are breathing exercises filling the gap? I think not.

Questions raised

- Does deep breathing really increase the volume and resonance of the voice?
- Does it increase speed in running, power in the kicking of a ball?
- Does extra air, and more specifically, extra oxygen, help us climb mountains?
- If you take over cortical control of the diaphragm, are you also prepared to take over cortical control of chemical balance throughout the body system?

All of the singing books that I have consulted in preparing this chapter advocate breathing exercises in direct relation to the activity of singing, in spite of the fact that breathing is for running *all* the body systems, not just singing. These exercises always include directions for using 'abdominal muscles, intercostal muscles and muscles of the lower

Voice training

back'. How many people not trained in physiotherapy or functional anatomy could identify which muscles they were using as they performed even simple tasks? The result in the student of singing, who will do anything to be able to sing, is to try hard. In other words do more than is required so as to be sure to 'get it right'. They breathe even deeper. They also tighten any muscles they are in touch with that lie below the waist – these being identified as 'abdominal'. These include those in the buttocks, which creates a chain reaction into leg muscles – the hamstrings and those in the front of the thigh – with potentially disastrous results to the voice.

Considering the evidence from Lum (1975), could over breathing be the key to performance nerves?

Could breathing exercises, which form such a major part of training for singing, be upsetting the body chemistry and reducing singing potential instead of accessing it?

Could singers be facing the same 'moderate hyperventilation' problems as patients in Lum's report? Imbalance in the body chemistry causes hypertension in smooth muscle. The pharynx is smooth muscle, which needs to be flexible to sing, breathe, and swallow.

Is lack of confidence, vocal tension, 'anxiety states' in performers, *caused* by a lack of training in up to date functional anatomy? Are these instructions familiar:

- "Take a few slow, deep breaths to settle your nerves"
- "Support the voice more on the breath"
- "Practice diaphragmatic breathing" (What can I say? How would you breathe without it?)

These phrases and hundreds like them in voice books published in the last two centuries give vague and often misleading instructions open to a variety of interpretations. But then, students of voice allow themselves to be instructed without questioning the how and the why. Maybe the lack of curiosity in the student allows outdated information to be continuously recycled.

What to do

To naturally increase respiratory response, go for a good brisk walk. That way the diaphragm will respond to demand, but a demand from the central nervous system, which is maintaining homeostasis over the whole diverse system. No wonder people have problems with singing a song if they are attempting to put the rest of themselves on hold while they do it. Any breathing exercises in people with no sign of pathology are suspect and so I never recommend any. Singing provides an opportunity for observation of the relationship between demand and efficiency and all your learning should use voice, body and right and left-brain.

All the exercises in *VoiceGym* link rotation, stretch and body strengthening in some way. These are all designed towards greater breathing efficiency, but not through amount. You should never take a breath to begin speaking or singing, but just begin to speak or sing at the maximum point of stretch and within the rhythm (see Chapter 10 - *Words and Rhythm*).

Imagine you have a fridge stocked with all that you need. You use some and *what you use is replaced, automatically* (Now wouldn't that be nice?). That is how your breathing system prevents over stocking. It replaces what you have used. Don't change that simply because you want to sing.

6. The importance of Tongue Position

Tongue position and Breathing

We are born with the whole tongue in the mouth, which allows us to breathe and suck at the same time (Crelin 1987). In the first few months this high and forward tongue position determines a high and forward position of the whole breathing/voice tract.

As upright posture is achieved and more demand is made on breathing and voice, the tongue, hyoid and the rest of the vocal tract descends to a lower position in the throat with the tongue now one third in the mouth and two thirds in the throat. It continues to descend throughout the years of two to six and by that age a stable relationship has been established between the position of the tongue, speech articulation, the development of the teeth and upright posture. This happens quite naturally with the gaining of language skills and lots of exercise.

Tongue position in the child

Between the ages of 2 and 6 the whole breathing and voice mechanism moves down the throat and vowels can now be articulated in the pharynx. After the age of 6 years old the position of the tongue, hyoid and larynx is determined by

- how efficiently, and how imaginatively, we use the voice;
- how much we sing;
- how we speak and how much;
- how much and how flexibly we move;
- how much demand we put on the breathing system.

Vocally and cranially, the human infant resembles the infant chimpanzee and can make only vowels and babbling noises: vocalising is restricted by the high position of the larynx. The relatively oversized tongue stimulates the nipple and also the growth and development of the roof of the mouth. This prepares the palatal arch for the developing dentition. After the first six months increased use of the voice and mobility of head and neck encourage further maxillary development, but, like the chimp with the similar skull, the infant cannot make consonant sounds because the tongue lies too far forward in the mouth. The importance of breast-feeding for the later good development of breathing,

STAGE I - Infant

The tongue is entirely in the mouth.

The primary function of the tongue is to suck.

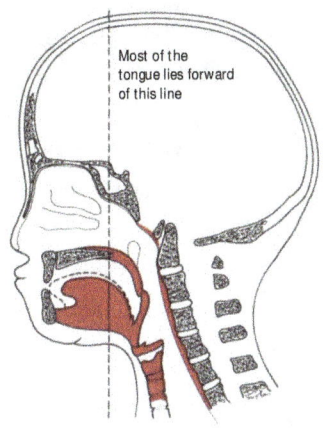

Most of the tongue lies forward of this line

STAGE II – From 2 to 6 years

The tongue and larynx drop back and down.

Speech is now possible.

Dotted positions of tongue, soft palate and throat muscles show the interactions that can now produce consonants.

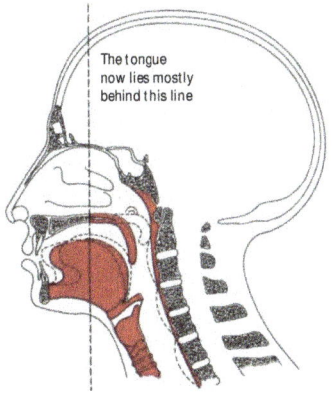

The tongue now lies mostly behind this line

STAGE III - Adult

Face and lip muscles articulate consonants and create facial expression.

Vowels are formed in the pharynx.

The dotted lines indicate articulation possibilities.

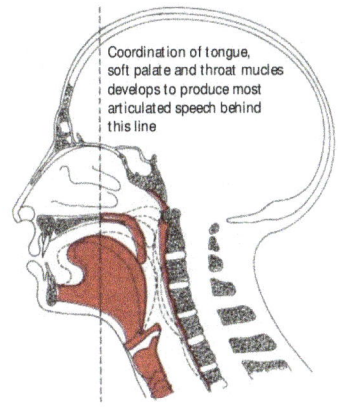

Coordination of tongue, soft palate and throat muscles develops to produce most articulated speech behind this line

Comparison of all three stages of tongue position. The tongue shifts from mostly in front of the dotted line to mostly behind it

voice, teeth, speech and posture cannot be stressed enough. The voice, body, right and left-brain are all involved in this process

All the natural drive the child displays between 2 and 6 is related, directly or indirectly to driving the larynx into its natural position, as low in the throat as possible, taking the tongue with it. These activities include

- balancing, on anything and everything
- jumping, skipping and generally bouncing around whenever possible
- climbing – trees, walls, gates, and fences – rather than taking the easy way round.
- Singing to any action which can be even loosely described as rhythmic
- Singing to anything repetitive and learned by rote.

So what is the natural position of the tongue now in relation to the mouth and in consequence, the face muscles that surround that area?

As the larynx descends the tongue must maintain its relationship with the hard palate as it is the action of the tongue in speech and in breathing that develops the width of this palate and ensures that there is enough space for the adult teeth when they finally appear. If this palate is not developed sufficiently the teeth will crowd. Prevention of crowding in the dentition is the job of the tongue.

The hard palate is the 'floor' of your breathing. Run the tip of your tongue backwards from your front teeth, along the centre of your hard palate to the soft palate, which hangs down behind it. This is the floor of your face and it has a line down its centre that you feel with your tongue tip, because the roof of the mouth is made up of two separate bones. The strong action of the tongue against this divide encourages bone growth and the palate expands from the centre.

To facilitate this good tongue work, which is also necessary for speech articulation, the tongue muscle strongly developed in breastfeeding continues to strongly balance the front third of the tongue against the hard palate.

On the Suspension Diagram at the beginning of Chapter 5 find the muscle that takes the tongue back and up towards the skull. This is called styloglossus.

This muscle connects the tongue backwards and upwards to the styloid process – the connection into the skull for the whole breathing and voice suspension. In fact, this muscle is part of that suspension.

Styloglossus gives the tongue a cobra-like action, being able to pull back and then spring forward. The strength of this muscle is an important factor in breathing efficiency

Balanced Tongue position and nose breathing

We are designed to breathe through the nose. Everything about the tongue and face muscles systems develops naturally towards that efficiency. If the styloglossus muscle that

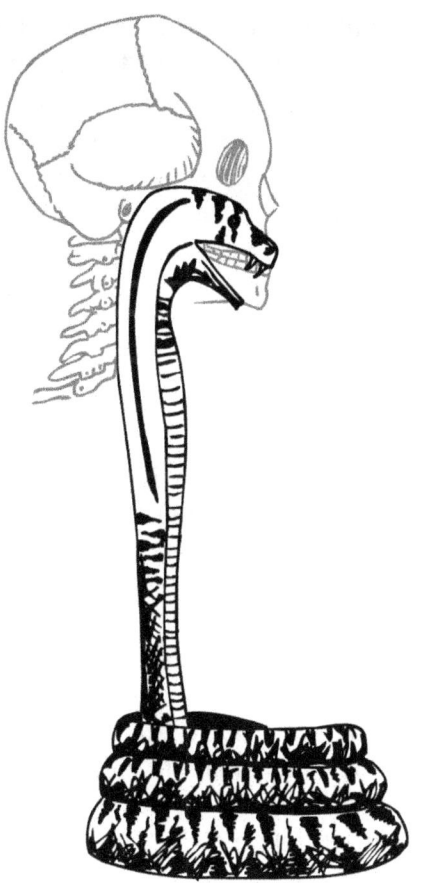

Tongue action is like that of the cobra striking. This is also a good illustration of your gut, where the tongue lives.

connects tongue and skull is weak, the tongue will not balance against the hard palate and may even fall into the floor of the mouth. The naturally balanced tongue forms a seal with the soft palate at the back of the mouth to prevent mouth breathing when the mouth is open. Think of all the times you open your mouth. When you smile and show your teeth; when you sing; when you talk; when you look up to paint the ceiling, etc. At those times a tongue collapsed into the floor of the mouth will change nose breathing into mouth breathing.

"But sometimes I need to breathe through my mouth! I want to sing a long phrase! I want to run fast, climb a mountain!"

There should never be a time when you are *only* mouth breathing. Efficient breathing is much more flexible than that. Nose breathing is the fundamental breathing system and it must never stop in favour of mouth breathing. If the body exerts itself and needs to supplement nose breathing by accessing air through the mouth, the tongue will break its seal at the back of the mouth just enough to provide that supplement. We are designed to nose breathe at all times except in emergency fight or flight. I leave you with that thought. Also this one…

There is a belief among singing teachers that a tongue resting against the palate closes off the pharynx. The tongue is generally encouraged to remain flat in the mouth at all times. If you watch a singer from the front the naturally articulating tongue will appear to fill the space you can see. But this is a working tongue articulating vowels in the pharynx and imploding rather than exploding consonants. There is maximum space in the pharynx when the tongue is in this position (See the diagram of vowel articulation in Chapter10).

Michael Macallion, who taught voice for the Royal Academy of Dramatic Art says in his book "The Voice Book", for actors, public speakers, and everyone who wants to make the most of their voice, "Don't allow the tongue to slide back down your throat – keep the tongue gently touching the lower front teeth". It would be difficult to prevent your tongue 'sliding down your throat'- it lives there.

The Alexander Technique and the Tongue

Glynn Macdonald, who teaches Alexander Technique at the Guildhall School of Music and Drama, LAMDA, and the Shakespeare Globe Theatre, says in her book *The Complete Illustrated Guide to the Alexander Technique,*

"Putting the tongue against the lower teeth is a preventative measure to help you stop contracting the back of the tongue and constricting the throat. It also creates a good antagonistic pull in that strong muscle. The tongue is the only muscle in the whole body connected directly to a bone (the hyoid) and exhibits a persistent tendency to over tighten and retract, not only restricting airflow, but creating a closed vocal tone that sounds strained".

Let me be quite clear. This is functionally misleading. The tongue is not one muscle, it consists of many different muscles, some voluntary, some involuntary, all of them working in different combinations to provide a multifactorial system of articulation, breathing, dental development and maintenance. Putting the tongue against the lower teeth gradually weakens styloglossus, changing the natural functional muscle programme of the face. The natural evolutionary development of tongue function illustrates, more than anything, the way specific disciplines have seen a miniscule view of the whole functional picture.

Why is nose breathing so important?

Air that is breathed through the nose passes through one of the best sterilization units ever developed. The nasal passages clean polluted air before it enters the vocal tract, thus protecting the delicate tissue of throat and lungs. The interior of the body is very warm and damp, an ideal environment for the growth of bacteria. When you breathe through the mouth polluted air has a free passage through the throat and into the lungs. As it is not the natural breathing system there is no filter on mouth breathing.

Air outside the body is not generally the same temperature as the inside of the body spaces, so it has to be brought to interior body temperature as part of inspiration for muscles to function efficiently. Imagine a sprinter having cold water poured over his legs before running his race. What do we do in cold weather? We hold ourselves tight together.

Breathing is not a breathe-in, breathe-out action like a bicycle pump. Between the nasal sinuses, where air is drawn in from outside, and the exchange of gases that happens in the lungs there is air in the pharynx. This is called the 'dead space', comprising the throat and the trachea. Air from the dead space will move first into the lungs and on breathing out all the air in the dead space areas must first be expelled before any from the lungs. (Guyton, 1977) A naturally balanced tongue, back and up against the palate, maintains the stability of the air that has been warmed and cleaned. A flat tongue allows the mouth to be part of that dead space, risking possible pollution from teeth or particles of food.

Ideally the tongue rests in a balanced position against the back of the hard palate. When the tongue is in this position -

- Air is breathed in through the nose
- Air is warmed and cleaned in the nasal passages.
- When the diaphragm contracts to move air into the lungs, the air in the' dead spaces', the throat spaces and the back of the mouth, which has been warmed to body temperature, flows into the lungs.
- The air from the sinuses, now sterile and with the chill off, moves into the dead spaces of the throat to acquire total body temperature before moving into the lungs with the next contraction of the diaphragm

Air breathed in through the mouth is cold, polluted, and lacks Nitric Oxide from the nasal passages, which is a key component in human health. Mouth breathing is bad for your health. The balanced position of the tongue is a major factor in your choice to breathe through your nose.

Are you beginning to realise what an amazing piece of chemical and mechanical engineering maintains the breathing system? Do you still want cortical control of it? A more worthwhile control would be to strengthen the natural resting position of your tongue, which determines whether or not you breathe efficiently through the nose.

When the tongue is allowed to fall forward in the mouth and rest against the bottom teeth, more than one third of the tongue is pulled into the mouth and the hyoid and larynx are unnaturally raised. The tongue is very heavy and this imbalance in tongue weight limits the downward excursion of the whole breathing/voice tract, narrows the throat, (pharynx) and turns natural effortless breathing into shallow, effortful breathing. Muscles of the upper chest are co-opted to provide the effort, drawing shoulders down and forward. The head will also take up a forward posture (Caine, 1998) In this effortful breathing most of the air will be drawn in through the mouth. This air has not been warmed or sterilized by passing through the nose.

Once again, efficient breathing comes back to the importance of maintaining a strong down spring of the larynx, hyoid and tongue, brought about by the flexibility of the suspensory mechanism. Balanced tongue weight is crucial for the efficiency and rhythm of this down spring.

This is a book to examine attitudes and training systems for the voice, but as the voice is the primary instrument from which all other musical instruments developed, the understanding of tongue position in relation to breathing is important, not only for all voice users, but for all musicians, whatever they play.

Your natural breathing rhythm dictates your phrasing. Where is your tongue when you play Beethoven Sonatas on the piano?

Flautists! How much muscle strength is there in the back spring of your tongue to provide 'tonguing' in the cadenzas of the Mozart D major concerto? Tonguing in any instrumental cadenza is dependant upon the strength and flexibility of the Styloglossus muscle. How's yours?

Brass players. A weak Styloglossus and a falling tongue will prevent the seal at the back of the mouth. Air will escape when you play.

Wherever I move in my thinking on breathing I come back to Guyton, Verigo, Buteyko, Lum and Yandell, who recognised that balance between CO_2 and oxygen was a crucial factor of efficient use of breath. The tongue makes nose breathing possible and efficient. If the tongue is not in the natural resting position up and back against the palate and does not act to close off the mouth you will breathe too much air in and blow too much CO_2, out, redering both 'tonguing' and breathing inefficient.

To correct this you may well then resort to breathing exercises!

7. Face Muscles

Breathing, speech, singing, chewing and swallowing all move the face. It also moves to smile, frown and perform other facial expressions.

One of the most important functions of the face muscles is to assist the tongue to maintain nose breathing

If the face and tongue muscles are developed with this priority, facial muscle balance will also develop naturally for speech, chewing, swallowing and facial expression. The face will also grow into a naturally shaped beautiful face. But it is not generally known how the face can change relative to the way you use the muscles. It is generally assumed that your face is "you" and will continue to be "you" throughout life. Cosmetic surgery is not the only means whereby you make changes.

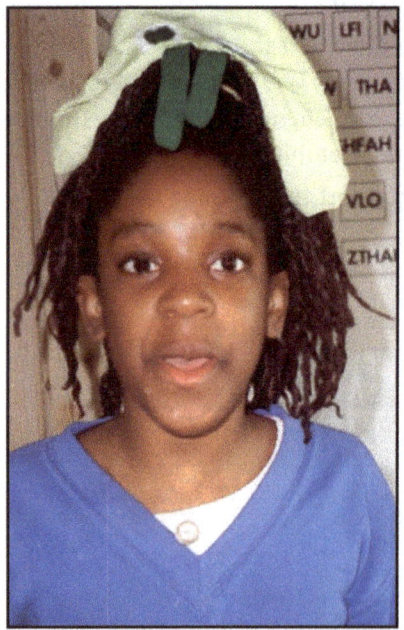
Sam before the exercise programme

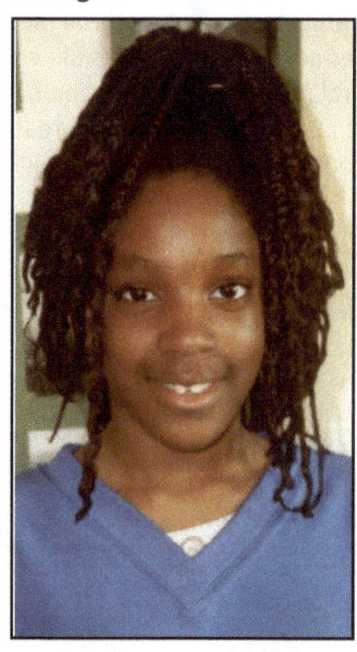
Sam four months later

Here is a picture of a little girl whose face was changed by exercising specific muscles and singing.

In the first picture she has a beanbag on her head to make her aware of how much she dropped her head back on her neck. She is wearing the same clothes in both pictures because that is the school uniform she always turned up in.

She came to me because she wanted to be in the school choir but she sang out of tune. She did an exercise programme to change her tongue position and you can see that the whole facial balance has changed. Not only did she sing in tune in the second picture, she is much prettier.

The next page has some photographs of people who all use their face muscles in the same way. They are all from different races and cultures, but all have what are universally accepted as beautiful features. It appears there are some common characteristics to 'beautiful' that also appeared in Sam after face and tongue exercise.

- Eyes are wide open and dominate the face
- Faces are wide across the eyes and narrow towards the chin
- The mouth is full and wide

In fact, width appears to dominate length in each of these faces. I believe this is due to the way the face muscles group when we use them, and that in many cases this may be less to do with genetics and more to do with early development.

This is an older face that has the same features as in the faces on the on the next page

- Eyes that dominate the face
- wide across the eyes and narrow towards the chin
- A full and wide mouth

All these faces display a priority for strong Group 1 muscles and a fully translating mandible (see Chapter 9)

This all suggests vitality; in the face and in the person

Beautiful women from around the world

"But I look like my mother/my father/ my Aunt Sally"
    Your family use their faces in a certain way, to talk, to chew, to teach you

basic skills and you copy, not only what to do, but the way their face reacts while they are doing it. When we are learning we need encouragement and we get that from the faces of those who teach us. A miserable looking teacher can wipe the smile off a child's face in five minutes and learning becomes an occupation that turns down the corners of the mouth and tightens the lips

"What are you smiling about? Get on with your work".

Stand in front of the mirror. You are about to give yourself a few muscle tests.

- Lift your upper lip in a sneer. This also dilates your nostrils.
- Lift one side of your upper lip, feeling the muscle ripple up the side of your nose, taking your nostril with it.
- Lift the other side of your lip the same way.
- Place all your fingertips along your cheekbone, with the index finger on the side of your eye. Lift this whole ark of your face with muscle. It will lift the upper half of your face and widen it.

If any of this is difficult, for instance if you can lift one side of your nose and not the other, get these muscles working. Use the car mirror when you are stuck in traffic. When the face doesn't respond push it with your finger until it does.

The muscles responsible for these actions are all voluntary, which means you can control them and a bit of what you have just been doing every day will soon alter the whole appearance of your face for the better, as well as increasing breathing through your nose (see Chapter 6- the Importance of Tongue Position)

Some people find it difficult and embarrassing to even discuss face muscles without becoming entangled with self image and personality, both of which include an awareness of how the face should look in relation to 'the self'. It is not generally understood how easily facial muscle balance can be changed by exercising specific muscles, in the same way that you may improve your waist measurement with special exercise and as a result, change your body shape.

First you must understand which muscles do what. This may seem too complicated to even consider, but functional anatomy is not difficult if you divide it up into levels. We will only consider level 1. You have your own working model to observe and try things out on if you can accept the idea that it is an exercise area like all others.

The face muscles can be divided into two groups.

Group 1 Muscles

These are concerned with nose breathing, swallowing, speech, singing and all the facial expressions of happiness, confidence and spontaneity.

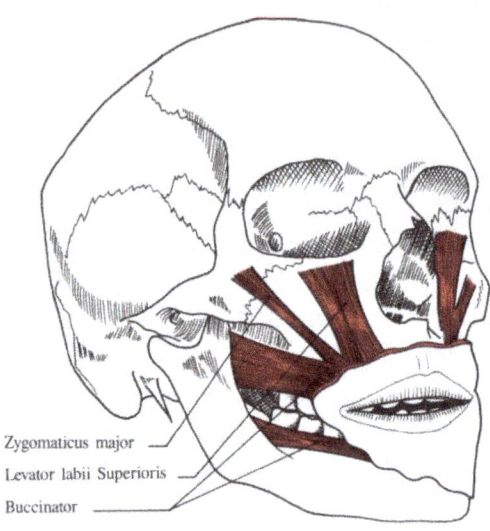

Zygomaticus major
Levator labii Superioris
Buccinator

Group 1 face muscles

They radiate from the centre of the face. They originate in bone and insert into moveable tissue.

On the inbreath the temporal bones on the sides of the skull and the central bones of the face move away from each other (minimally!). This is one moment in the 'wave' motion of the sacro-cranial rhythm. You may not feel it and you certainly will not see it. Remind yourself of its importance by revisiting chapter 1 development.

The action of Group1muscles encourages the cranium to widen in the facial area and flare the nostrils. This reduces pressure throughout the nasal cavities and maxillary sinuses, and as a result the outside air moves into the nasal sinuses. The air can then be warmed, cleaned and sterilised before the contraction of the diaphragm and opening of the glottis of the larynx pulls air from the dead space of the pharynx into the lungs. Imagination and emotion can extend this action into a smile; further still into laughter. These muscles stretch the skin of the face in an upward and outwards direction, thus widening the whole facial aspect. This is following the model of beauty that is so universally accepted.

Group 2 Muscles

These act in the vertical plane to chew. For strength and purchase they originate in bone and insert into bone, and they have more bulk and less delicacy than Group 1.

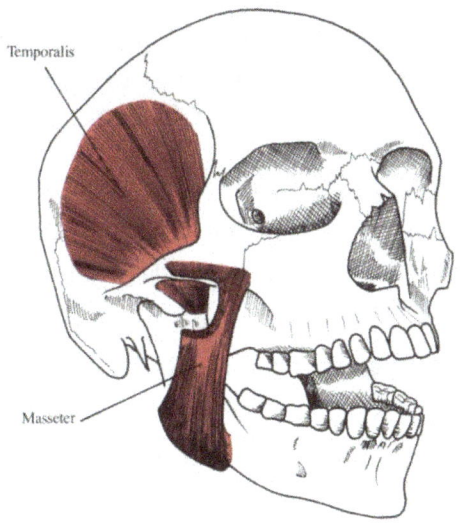

Group 2 Face Muscles

The Temporalis muscles snap the teeth together and masseter applies a vertical force to crush food against the molar facets (aided by lateral movement from the Pterygoid muscles, not shown). These muscles generally have no function in breathing, speech, singing, or swallowing apart from a few anterior fibres of the Temporalis muscle (emphasised) that suspend the mandible in a position to facilitate independent action of the tongue in articulation of speech Chapter 9.

Group 2 Muscles are activated when the tongue takes up a forward and down position to push food between the teeth: the lips are firmly closed to keep the food in. The mouth must be closed to chew, but closing is not necessary for nose breathing.

When tongue action is efficiently balanced, and the tongue suspended at the back of the mouth, it is the seal between tongue and soft palate that determines whether you breathe through the nose. Pressing the lips together and vacuuming in air through the nose merely interferes with facial muscle balance and narrows the nostrils. Scowling and sulking and other expressions associated with unhappiness are involuntary expressions of Group 2 muscles (Caine, 1995).

Experiment 1: back to the mirror

Press your lips together. Your tongue immediately comes forward and down to rest against your teeth. Try to move your jaw, smile or breathe through your nose and discover how you have restricted facial expression and movement of the jaw. You can only 'vacuum' in air, narrowing the nostrils.

We are not intended to live with the mouth open and risk infection, or choking, but balanced face function results in the mouth gently and effortlessly resting closed with equal fullness in upper and lower lips (Caine, 1991).

Swallowing and what you can learn from it

The top of the throat, just behind the mouth, is a descending tube that opens into the mouth. It is attached to the face at a line of thick, stiff connective tissue (the Pterygoid Raphe). The position of the Pterygoid Raphe is determined by the action of the Buccinator muscle.

When food enters the mouth, the Buccinator muscle contracts and pulls the Pterygoid raphe forward, (see diagram). The first constrictor of the pharynx also moves forward and the throat space is reduced, reducing danger of food accidentally passing into it and the danger of choking.

The contraction of the Buccinator muscle pushes the food between the molars from the cheek area while the tongue works in the floor of the mouth to push the food back between the molars from inside the dental arch. When the food is reduced sufficiently by chewing, the throat needs to expand to allow fast passage of the food down the throat and safely past the airway. This swallowing action is fundamental to the articulation of speech.

Experiment 2

Have a mouthful of something to chew and swallow – not too dry or chewing is difficult, what about an apple? Notice that you are using the strong muscles on the sides of your cheeks to chew – masseter - and that any sideways action comes, not from the front of the face, but from behind the jaw – the Pterygoids. Notice that your tongue is forward and down. When you are ready to swallow, pause for a moment in neutral. When you swallow notice that you use the Group 1 muscles. Your tongue goes up and back and the whole of the front of the face lifts a little as if in a smile. This is Buccinator shifting the Pterygoid raphe to open the throat. Next time you watch a trumpeter play watch for the action of Buccinator. It is the trumpeter's muscle (unless it is Dizzy Gillespie who broke every rule in the trumpet manual and puffed out his cheeks).

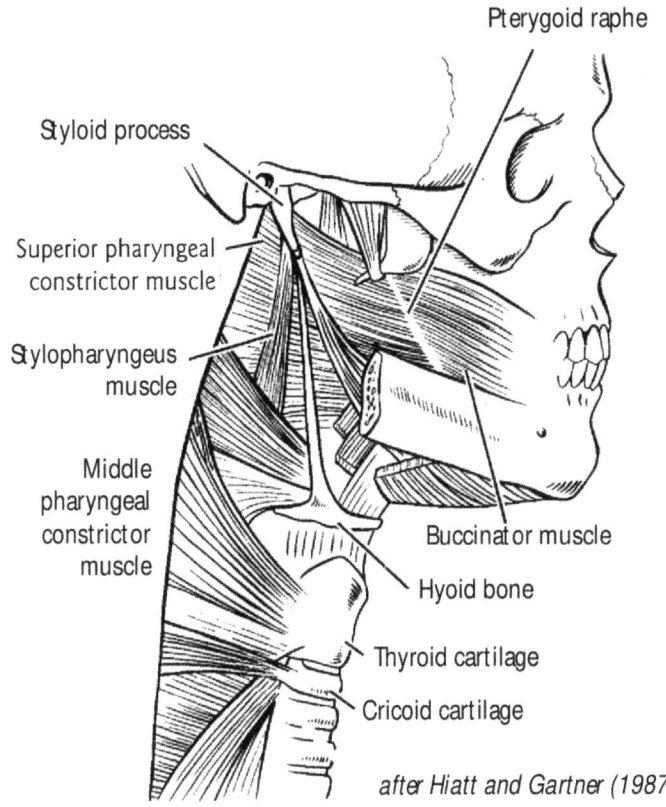

after Hiatt and Gartner (1987)

In the functions of swallowing, nose breathing, singing and speech the Buccinator muscle will position the Pterygoid Raphe posteriorly so as to facilitate maximum space in the superior constrictor.

If -

- At school, you have been told to "wipe that smile off your face and get on with your work".
- You have worn a dental appliance on our teeth at some time and kept your upper lip down to cover it, pressing your lips together.
- You are in a profession that necessitates low response to panic. The police officer, paramedic, nurses, doctor, lawyer, are obvious, but what about the teacher who has to deal with major discipline problems, or the parent who has to remain calm when your son has written off your one and only vehicle?
- You feel dissatisfied, unfulfilled, and unhappy with your lot.

You may spend much of your life with a facial priority for muscle group B. This strengthens muscle Group B and very soon Muscle Group A is unavailable. Your face is now looking long and narrow.

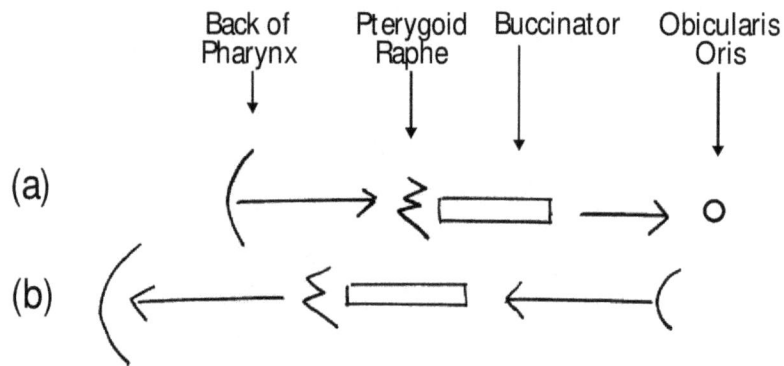

The Role of Buccinator

In chewing, Buccinator will act in relation to Obiculoris Oris, positioning the Pterygoid Raphe anteriorly.

This will help to shape your face for both beauty and efficient nose breathing.

Reprogramming your lip area changes the way the Buccinator muscle behaves as is shown in the diagram on the previous page. The Pterygoid Raphe is pulled posteriorly, increasing the throat space for swallowing, talking, singing and breathing. Any activity which demands maximum efficiency in breathing, rhythmic coordination and power needs to prioritise the face muscles of Group 1.

A smiling face and relaxed full lips which lift easily and naturally off the upper teeth is the mark of:
- the successful runner, singer, wind player, dancer or skater,
- the beautiful face,
- self-confidence.

The Sucking Reflex

I cannot leave the area of the face without repeating that early development lays down patterns that we have to deal with for all of our lives. While you are reading the next bit, tap the area between lips and nose lightly about twelve times. Now stop and read on. You have been stimulating the area of your sucking reflex. It develops in-utero, and we need a strong sucking reflex for the period when we are totally dependant on breast-feeding. It pops up in our lives when we crave comfort: sucking pencils, our fingers, pens and lollipops, smoking, pursing the lips, biting the lips and the nails.

Can you still feel sensation in your upper lip? The sucking reflex is very strong and when stimulated, remains stimulated a long time. It is always with us. It is important to remember that when we sucked, we did not have the power of speech. Excessive stimulation of the sucking reflex may reduce speech potential because with the lips pursed you just don't feel like talking or singing.

Think of using the Group 1 facial muscle group to widen across the cheekbones and maintain maximum throat space for breathing, singing and speech.

Keep doing the muscle experiment at the beginning of the chapter to check the strength of these movements.

8. Balance and Posture

You are an upright biped of over 200 separate bones and the relationship of those bones must be maintained in a reasonably balanced stack if you are not to fall over. For this reason many bones and muscles are paired to exert equal weight and equal pull in opposite directions, but if the basic skeletal structure of bones (skeleton) and teeth (the way they bite together) loses this integrity, extra muscle effort is co-opted to maintain upright posture. This reduces efficiency in the whole system, creating stiffness in movement and weakness in muscle groups where one muscle fails to support a chain of movement. Muscles are often diverted from their natural position in the muscle chain to prevent injury somewhere else.

The voice reflects misalignment of the physical structure (Caine, 1996).

This is the information that changed my thinking about the cause of most voice problems.

In 1960, Wolfgang and Adolph Zenker tested the hypothesis that the extrinsic muscular frame (the vocal suspension) that supported the larynx affected the voice. Their conclusion was that these muscles were influential, particularly on pitch making. When the larynx was in a position of rest, activity in these muscles was minimal, but any action of the larynx– breathing, speaking,

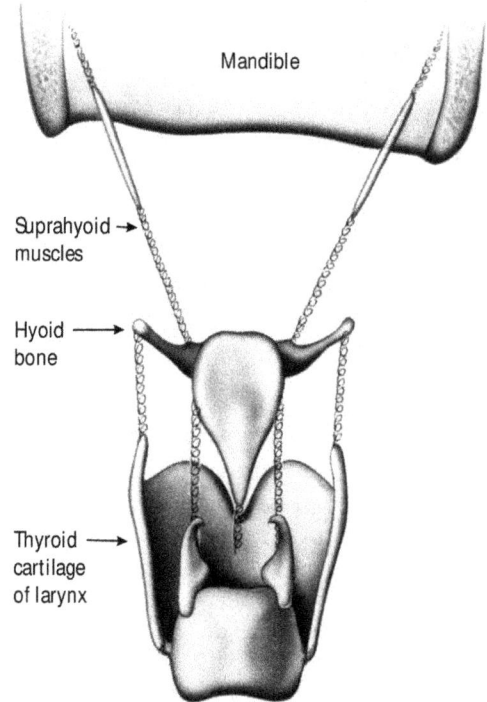

The springs represent muscle connections. There is an obvious muscle connection from the interior of the larynx to the Mandible. If the mandible is involved, so is the whole head and neck (after Fink and Demarest, 1978).

swallowing, singing – brought about a corresponding reaction in the extrinsic muscular frame. "Thus this system (the larynx) is greatly influenced by respiration (breathing), posture and the position of the jaw and tongue".

In other words –

- Breathing/voice, posture/balance, jaw and tongue are interactive through the extrinsic muscular frame, which links them all together.

This is the link.

Figures 1 and 2 on the next page are illustrations from Jonathon Howat's book 'Chiropractic'. They illustrate categories of misalignment regularly treated by a chiropractor. Figure 2 clearly shows a shift in body posture that will misalign the vocal suspension.

It is easy to see that if the vocal suspension in the Fink and Demarest diagram were superimposed on Howat's second diagram of asymmetrical spinal distortion, as a result of this posture unequal pulls in the muscular suspension would occur in the extrinsic muscular frame even when the larynx was in a position of rest. Every down spring of the larynx in breathing, swallowing, speech and singing would be affected by the posture of the head, neck and mandible, which are all skewing over to one side.

- in the temporal bones of the skull, from which the larynx is suspended;
- in the Hyoid, which is connected to each shoulder blade by the Omohyoid muscle – one now shorter than the other (see diagram on Page 44);
- of the two jaw joints, which are housed in the temporal bones;
- of the main articulator – the tongue, which connects back and up to the styloid process of the skull.

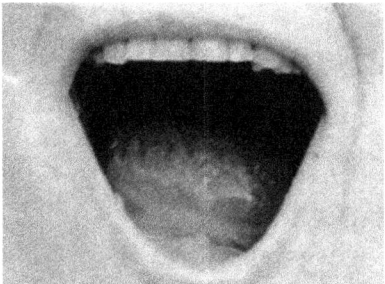

This is a photograph of a tongue when styloglossus muscles from misaligned temporal bones are pulling it back and up to connect with the soft palate (see Chapter 6 - *The importance of tongue position*).

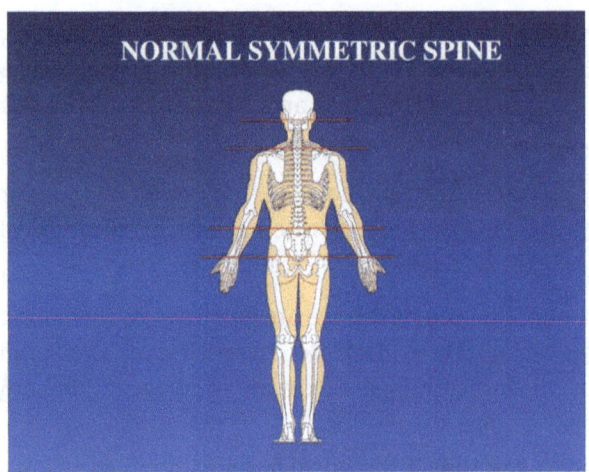

Figure 1: Naturally balanced posture

What causes the skeletal shift from Figure 1 to Figure 2? Is this the result of an accident?

Of course it could be. For example, when you break a limb you shift your weight away from the painful area. You use the damaged limb as little as

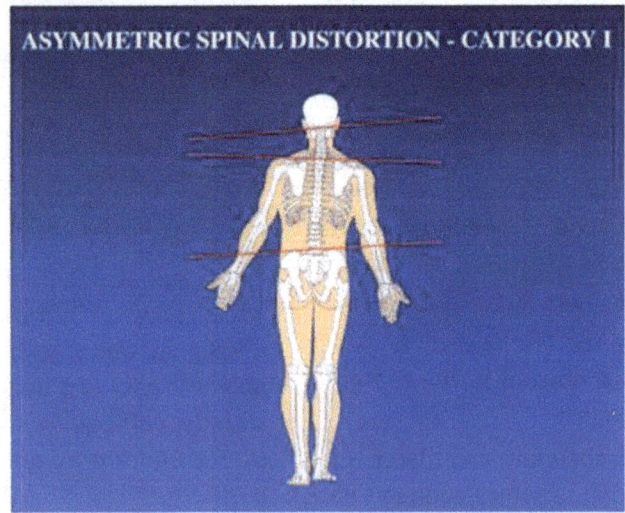

Figure 2: Category 1 misalignment
Both reproduced from Howat (1999)

After the limb has healed it is still weak so you may continue to use the emergency muscle system you have co-opted. You may get used to this system and begin to feel it is 'normal'. Eventually, if you don't return to the normal pre-injury function, this muscle system will begin to create its own problems.

This is where physiotherapy and exercise help to return the body to efficient posture and movement. Returning the muscles to natural function is all part of the recovery process.

Less obvious, but more common in the general population is the lack of regular maintenance for day-to-day upright postural balance. We stand up at roughly one year old to the delight of proud parents. Within quite a short time we are steady on our feet and walking everywhere. This period lays the foundation of balance for the rest of our lives. Consider how little time we have to learn this, how long we have to use it and how little maintenance it gets.

Message to parents

When your toddler struggles upright don't bring out the baby walkers and 'push-alongs'. We can all balance if we hold on. It is better that the process of learning to walk is slow and full of attempts that end up 'plop', down on the bottom once again.

Momentum aids balance. Tottering along unaided helps us to discover how to stay upright with little momentum to help. Toddlers love to crawl up the stairs and anything else they can get onto. They totter for a bit and then crawl up the stairs, which strengthens the back. Small children instinctively know what they need to develop the upright biped. Next time, the totter is a bit stronger. Be behind, of course, when they crawl up the stairs.

Once we are on our feet all the natural activities of playing with balance strengthen that central core of stability with paired bones, paired muscles. We learn that balance is not just two dimensional, but multidirectional. There are many other ways to topple over besides backwards or forwards. We learn all the movements before six years old and then we use this vocabulary of movement to build complex activities, much as the voice practices sounds, down spring, rhythm and a priority for vowels and then uses that vocabulary to develop complex speech and reading patterns. All fundamental systems come together about six years old (Chapter1 - *Early Development*).

This balancing practice must continue when we go to school, not just in riding bikes, skateboards, roller-blades – these all have momentum to aid balance. Children need to walk and play in natural areas where running, skipping, rolling about and climbing emphasizes where 'centre' is. Ropes that swing you from trees, tyres that swing you and spin you, all develop and maintain multidirectional balance and co-ordination by giving you a sense of where the middle of you is.

Homo sapiens are not designed to operate in two dimensions, but is a multidirectional creature. Postural balance which maintains upright posture:

- balances the vocal suspension, opening up possibilities of singing and all other musical activities;
- balances doing, thinking, moving, observing, talking and listening.

The balance of this extraordinary biped is based on a paired muscle system, but that paired muscle system does not merely move us forward and backwards; to the left or right. It has a secret ingredient.

Rotation and Torque

Torque – the movement of a system of forces, tending to cause rotation

John the Baptist (Leonardo de Vinci, Circa 1508)

Watch any human movement and you will see the body rotate as it moves. This has been studied since the work of the first anatomist – Leonardo de Vinci.

Leonardo was fascinated by the action of spiralic movement. By introducing spirals into his drawings of water, animals, people and drapery he discovered a way to make his drawings move. Water tumbled, horses pranced, and sleeves fell from poised arms. When this spiralic action was introduced into painting human anatomy, faces smiled and forms expressed emotion. But he soon discovered that this was not merely a technique of drawing and painting. The bones he dug up were curved and their shapes projected into spirals. He found that muscles were arranged across joints so that a right arm stretched out created a spiral that arose in the opposing left hip, crossed the back diagonally, wound under the right armpit, down the front of the right arm and pointed backwards at the sky from the right thumb.

In 1968 Raymond Dart described the double spiral arrangement of the body musculature, which wraps around the body in two opposing spiral sheets. All humans have this spiralic arrangement of muscle. It provides the human body with the twisting actions so characteristic of the skilled dancer, gymnast, or sportsperson.

Every movement is based on extension or flexion of these opposing spiralic sheets and true poise is based on the perfect opposition of this double spiral. Most of us compromise this balance and poise by developing movements that are asymmetrical, that is, favour the strengthening of a right or left torsion. Remedial exercises for faulty posture are only given when that compromise reaches the end of adaptation and pain is experienced. By then posture will not be considered as the fundamental problem, exercise is unlikely to address the spiralic postural muscle system, only the symptomatic and localised problem of pain.

Most of the *VoiceGym* exercises encourage balanced posture and the rotational pulls in the human musculature. Part 3 concentrates on building strength in both muscle spirals and ensures that using the voice does not become a two dimensional activity.

The physio-ball exercise programme provided with *VoiceGym* also works balance as well as stretch, thus making sure that both spirals are working evenly.

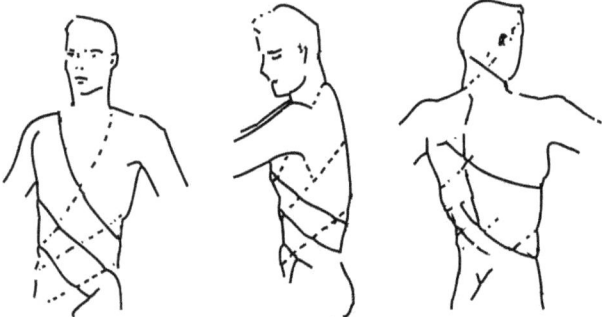

Raymond Dart saw the muscle system of the torso as two separate and balanced spiral sheets (after Dart, 1968)

The Head

The double spiralling sheets of muscle illustrated above begin at the front bony edge of the pelvis on each side and after spiralling around the whole trunk, insert into the large bony lump on the base of the skull, just behind the ear. This is the mastoid process of the temporal bone. This bone has already been identified as housing

- the styloid process, from which the whole breathing/voice mechanism is suspended,
- the joint between jaw and skull: the temporo-mandibular joint,
- the vestibular canals of the ear responsible for upright postural balance.

It has also been identified the most likely part of the skull to suffer acute compression during the birth process.

A line drawn across the base of the skull from one mastoid process to the other goes through the fulcrum of the lever system, which balances the head on the spine. The action of the double spiral muscle system acts upon and is conversely acted upon by the balance of the head on the neck. The movement of the eyes is the prime mover of this system, followed by movement of the head. The rest of the body is swung from the head by means of the two spirally arranged muscle sheets, much as our fishy and amphibian ancestors moved through the water. We tend to think in terms of the head being poised on the spine. To adopt the attitude that the eyes and head lead the rest of the body is to access greater freedom of movement and a more balanced symmetry.

The Alexander Technique, developed by F M Alexander uses the principle of 'the head leading body movement' to re-educate the body to move in a more balanced and effortless way.

The Waist

The crossover of the double spiral muscle system forms the waist. The thickening of your waist is one of the first signs of postural weakness. To restore the waist one must build up the tone of the oblique muscles by stretching the opposing spiral sheets. How are yours?

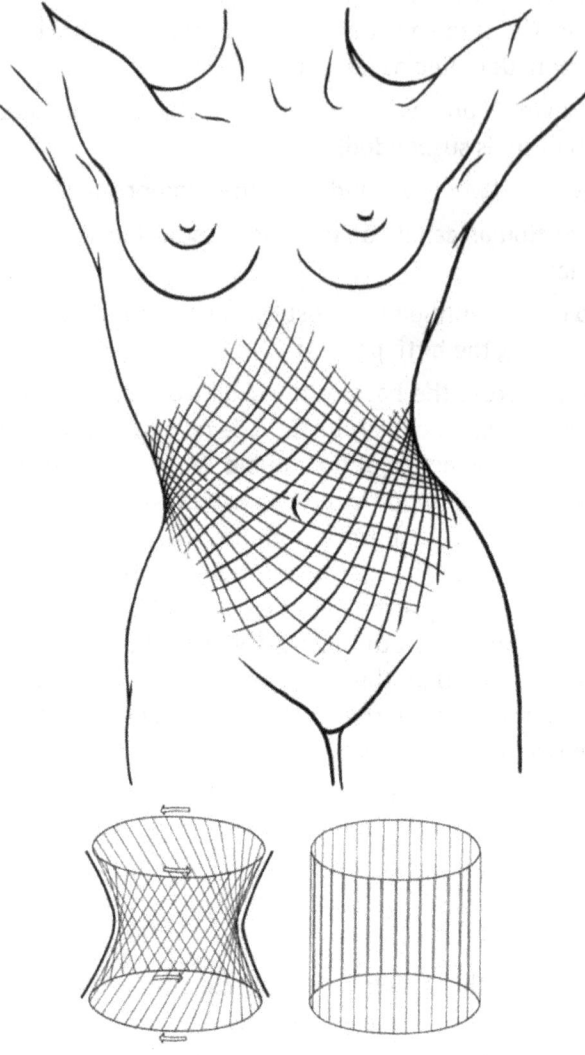

Reproduced from Kapandji, (1970)

Gaudi, the Barcelona architect, experimented with achieving curves in concrete, rotating the stress-bearing columns to produce the 'branches' that support the roof of his Church of the Sacred Family. From Leonardo to the present day, Principles of strength through torsion have taken the human body as the model of action and reaction, creating architectural wonders based on strengthening by 'torque'.

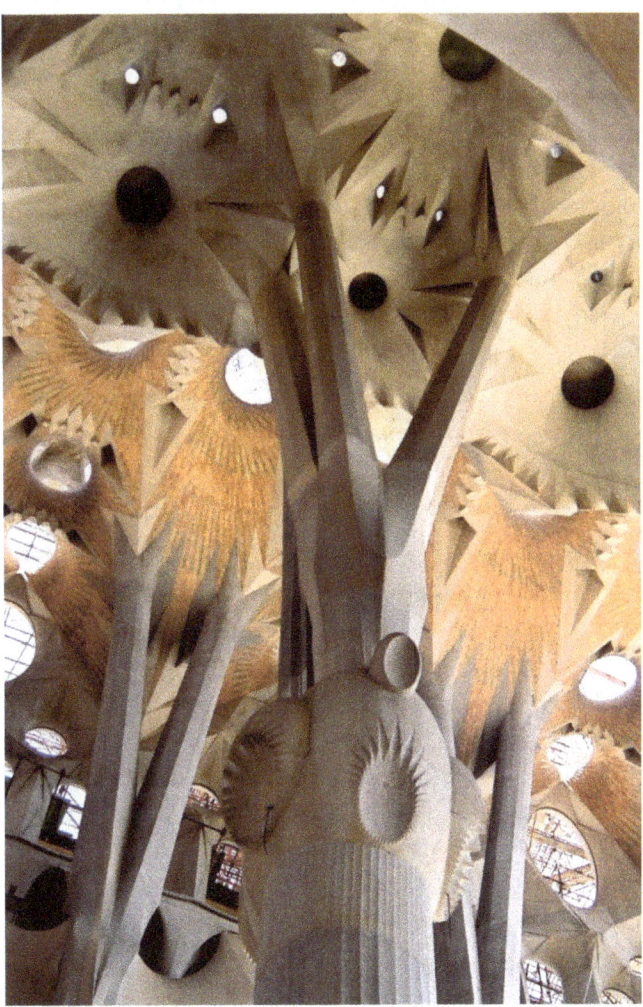

The roof of the partly completed Church of the Holy Family in Barcelona, which was conceived by the architect Gaudi

Hands

One of the human tools that fascinated Leonardo was the hand. As a painter, engineer, sculptor and musician the hand was crucial in his own life and he must have seen its importance to him every day.

In 1982 Kapandji devoted almost half of the pages of 'The upper Limb' in his 'The Physiology of the Joints' to the hand, because " the hand is not only a motor organ but also a very sensitive and accurate sensory receptor, which feeds back information essential for its own performance. Finally it provides the cerebral cortex with information regarding thickness and distance and thus is responsible for the development of visual appreciation by allowing cross checking of information. Without the hand our idea of the world would be flat and lacking in contrasts. It trains the brain in the appreciation of texture, weight, and temperature. By itself, unaided by the eye, the hand is able to recognise an object.

The hand therefore forms with the brain an inseparable interacting functional pair and it is this close interaction that is responsible for man's ability to alter nature at will and to dominate other species".

"What am I to do with my hands when I perform/present/sing?"

When the body is well balanced, hand, eye and voice enjoy a good relationship. The hand subtly enhances, by gesture, what the voice is expressing. When there is a lack of co-ordination between hand and voice, gesture is awkward, inappropriate and often too much.

The shoulder blades are the anchorage and counterweight for the bone mass of the shoulder girdle, arms and hands. When you raise your hand the shoulder blade and its muscle attachments behave like the counterweight in the lift and the hand gesture moves out from a state of balance, not a body precipitating forwards. Leaning forward in a presentation or singing performance tenses the pharynx, arms and hands and gesture will then be awkward. The omohyoid muscle links hyoid bone and shoulder blade: find it in Chapters 1 and 6. Voice, arm and hand are linked on the same muscle chain. Balance of the upper body is fundamental to presentation, singing or teaching.

A two dimensional life

Balanced, multidirectional posture is not generally considered to be a necessary life skill to acquire. Development of efficient posture is not included in education or training, in spite of the fact that many hard working professions have to deal constantly with demand that pulls them off balance. Doctors, dentists, surgeons, hairdressers, teachers, counsellors, mothers of small children, dedicated directors of companies, gardeners, computer operators, lawyers, will eventually develop a forward posture unless there is regular maintenance of upper body to stabilise the shoulder girdle by exercising the muscles responsible for maintaining erectness of posture.

Constant leaning forward results in forward shoulder posture, followed by forward tongue posture and collapse of the lateral face muscles in favour of the vertical chewing system (Chapter 7 - *Face Muscles*). When the shoulder girdle collapses forward the hands become 'over-busy'.

How do we become two-dimensional?

There are many other ways. The seating arrangements in schools, training courses and the work place are about 'getting your head down and getting on with it'. This is good for completing set tasks, but not for having original ideas. Regular breaks, some with a really good stretch and a sing, (especially with movement) would revitalise learning potential and stimulate the group/class to be more vocal. It would encourage discussion and questions, rather then the pattern of 'the teacher has the information – I am here to learn it by sitting quietly and absorbing it'. These goals and aims often encourage two-dimensional thinking, like...

- Are you moving forward in your career? Or are you falling back?
- Did you pass or fail your exams?
- Are you right handed or left-handed?
- Are you for or against this or that political agenda?
- Are you academic? Or practical?
- Musical? Or unmusical?

'Either-or' is two-dimensional thinking and two-dimensional thinking goes with two-dimensional upright posture: limiting movement to either forward or backward.

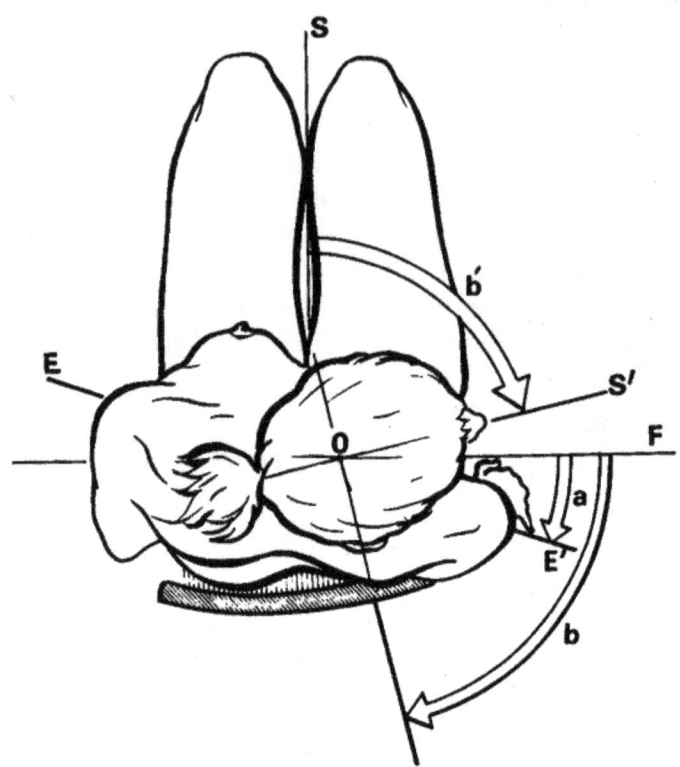

Rotational possibilities in the spine are
best viewed from above (after Kapandji, 1974)

The spine itself is designed for rotation and remains healthy with rotational exercise. Chairs which wheel about and roll around encourage the sitter to be still and two dimensional, while the chair provides the means of rotating and reaching around you. Backs strengthen with exercise, not a support system that *prevents* exercise. Constant sitting is in itself an encouragement to postural collapse, but why add a 'wheelchair' to someone with no pathological condition?

When this happens it is time to revitalise your double spiral arrangement. Any exercise that twist your pelvis one way and your shoulder girdle and ribs the other will do.

The range of rotation of the vertebral column as a whole is best observed from above by fixing the pelvis and knees and turning the head. I am sure you can repeat the experiment and discover your own rotation possibilities. If they do not match this maybe you should consider a backless stool at your office desk and a physio ball at your computer!

The Feet

This is the place where total body weight arrives on the earth – or does not.

Like the palms of our hands, the bottom of the feet is particularly sensitive. Your feet need to *feel* the different surfaces you walk upon. Take off your shoes, stand in front of a full-length mirror and look at how you stand. Scan yourself from top to toe and back again and then tell yourself that for efficient posture your weight should be evenly distributed over the tripod of your feet; heels, big toe joint, little toe joint. When you remember this, do you have to move back on your heels because you are too far forward?

What are your feet doing? How far apart are they?

Stand with feet absolutely parallel and hip joint width apart, knees soft but not bent. This allows your body weight pass through the legs and onto the ground.

Hip joint width apart – what is that?

Your hip joints are roughly halfway between where you put your hands on the outside of your upper thigh and your groin. Your heels should be underneath this point. You may feel really uncomfortable in standing at first – a bit like a duck, but tell yourself that the greatest expense in the NHS is hip replacement and knee replacements aren't far behind. Standing with feet under hip joints lines up ankle, knee, and hip in a better way.

What moves first when you step forward?

Your knee should break out from under your hip with minimal lateral sway. If there is a big lateral sway as you move forward, your feet are too far apart when you stand. Check this in a full-length mirror.

Important points

- Each foot has 26 bones and each hand has 26 bones. Your hands and your feet contain one third of your bone structure. Keep hands and feet separately exercised for total flexibility.
- The brain operates on a feedback system called proprioception. Joints house more proprioceptors (individual sensors that provide this feedback) than muscle. Joints provide the majority of feedback from body to brain, so movement is better than sitting still.
- The hands and feet provide one third of the feedback system to the brain about you in space, upright balance, the state of the surrounding world, where everything else is, where you are. Start stretching hands and feet.
- You may spend all day in shoes, probably the same shoes, so that your feet are receiving the same message whatever surface you tread. This does not stimulate postural reflexes. You will become tired very easily. Do you really _use_ your hands? Do you make things, mend things, ever write with a pen, draw, and sew? Or are your hands as limited as your feet?

It is recommended that you revisit your feet. Take off your shoes whenever possible, not just to save someone's carpets, but to save your own structural integrity. If you learn to live without shoes and leave them by the back door, do not put them on again to go down the garden to hang up the washing or to go out and empty the kitchen bin. Step on the odd stone, feel the different surfaces. A bit of "OO" and "Ouch" wakes up your feet and tests your balance.

Trainers

The feet are your contact with the earth and with gravity. The sensors in your feet do not work without stimulus. With a wedge of cushioning between heel and ground you literally do not know where you are in space and the feet have no spring. Lacking spring and postural reflex shoulders may collapse forward   Eventually this will affect the postural spiral muscle chain, breathing, the voice in singing and speech and thus personal power.

Originally trainers were sports shoes designed to add speed in running to efficient feet in a body already developed in natural postural integrity, with all muscle systems strengthened and in balance. They have become an image shoe that targets the population with the message that wearing an expensive trainer will give you a better body image. In small children this hinders the natural development of balance.

Trainers are for those who can already run, dance, jump, skip or climb. A good training shoe will improve the strength that you have already built into the system. You will only really gain if you first of all develop your own unaided skills.

Posture is not about standing up straight

You encountered a system of springs in Chapter 1. Movement, rhythm, down spring and rebound all co-ordinate these springs and the spiral muscle system. These are all terms that should be associated with the word 'posture'. Balance is the relationship of bones and muscles in space, but just thinking of standing up straight is dead anatomy. We must move to fulfil our role in the scheme of things.

Look at the trampoline in Chapter 1 - *Practical Working Model*. Imagine that when you hit the centre of the mat, one corner of the frame gave way a little. What would happen to your somersault then?

9. Jaws and Teeth

The dentist is given full responsibility for making all decisions concerning jaws and teeth, sometimes planning orthodontic work that costs thousands. The orthodontist that carries out that work may never have consulted any other structural clinician or you as the patient. Yet what happens when the teeth come together can affect the balance of the whole body by changing the relationship between masses like the head and neck, or the spine and pelvis.

When I am consulted about voices that have begun to show dentally related stress I always ask, "Did you get a second opinion before you agreed to this?"

The answer is always "No, why should I. The orthodontist is the expert?"

If your car is damaged the insurance company will require two quotes and the relative reports before agreeing to pay for one of them and your car is a piece of machinery that can be replaced. You have only one of you and it is your responsibility to take care of, and responsibility for, yourself. The doctor, dentist, orthodontists or anyone else you consult is giving you the benefit of their advice, which you must ensure is the best advice available, not merely the best advice available to that particular consultant.

Many dentists and orthodontists have already recognised that they affect much more than merely the area they work in and have formed study groups and organisations that encourage networking with other clinical disciplines. There are dental practices where an 'in-house' cranial osteopath or chiropractor will discuss openly with the dentist and the patient a mutually agreed treatment protocol. That orthodontist may personally advise a second opinion in order to secure your complete co-operation. Informed co-operation in the patient ensures that everyone is confidently working towards the same known result. Treatment success is unlikely without al of these factors.

This chapter is to give you some very basic information so that you feel you are in a position to ask sensible questions of your dentist. If your dentist does not like being questioned about the treatment plan he has for you, get another dentist. It is much easier and less expensive than attempting to recover your voice, replace your lost teeth, or correct serious and debilitating back pain, all of which can be caused by inappropriate orthodontic treatment, at any age. From now on I will use technical terms, all of which appear in the glossary. This will give you more confidence when talking to your dentist, and conversations between clinicians will not go over your head.

The Mandible

Where is it?

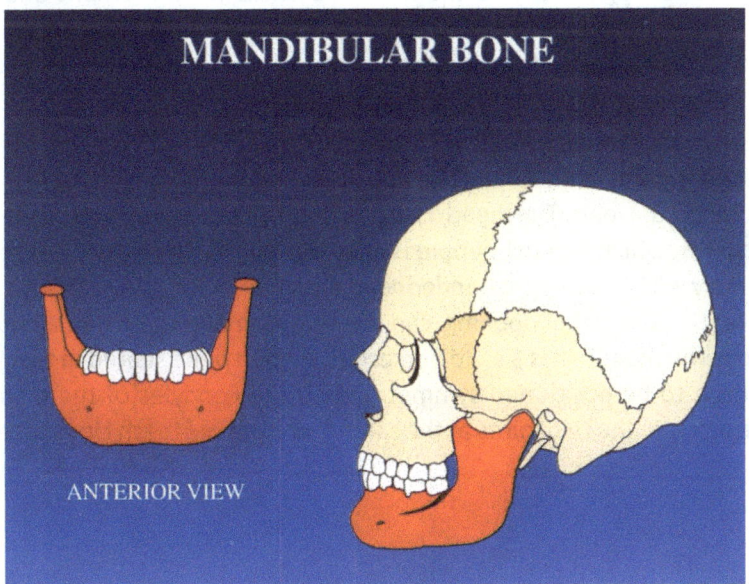

Reproduced from Howat (1999)

Sit in front of a mirror to help the following observations

Find the TMJ (Temporo-Mandibular Joint) on yourself. Poke around just in front of your ear while moving the jaw from side to side. This will locate the joint – the jaw moves, the skull remains still.

Put an index finger in each ear with the palm of your hand facing forward. Smile broadly. Press the finger against the front of your ear-hole and in this position you can listen to the movement of the joint as you very slowly open your mouth a wide as possible and then close it as slowly as possible. Smile broadly before you do this and keep the smile throughout. Now repeat the movement in front of a mirror and watch the movement of the mandible as it opens and closes. There are several possible discoveries from this test:

- Clicking, grinding, or other internal noises on one side or on both sides indicate that the mandible does not translate - move in relation to the joint - as freely as it could.
- Uneven travel, a swing of the mandible to one side or the other shows that muscles moving the mandible, or ligaments supporting the mandible are working unevenly, stronger on one side than the other.
- A sudden 'jiggle' where the mandible sticks for a moment and then releases, maybe with an accompanying click could indicate that the capsular disc within the joint is under compression or even displaced.

It has already been shown that postural muscles spiral around the body to insert finally into the mastoid process of the temporal bone, just behind the ear. Find this bony lump. The temporal bone also houses the TMJ, just in front of the ear. The head is balancing on the spine and leading all movement, which in most people is in favour of a slight right or left torsion to comply with left or right handedness. A mandible swinging slightly to one side or the other on opening can be symptomatic of a more extreme torsion. The mandible is a solid horseshoe shaped bone seated in two joints that have to be positioned symmetrically if the condyles of the mandible are to arrive in the two joints at the same time that the teeth close together.

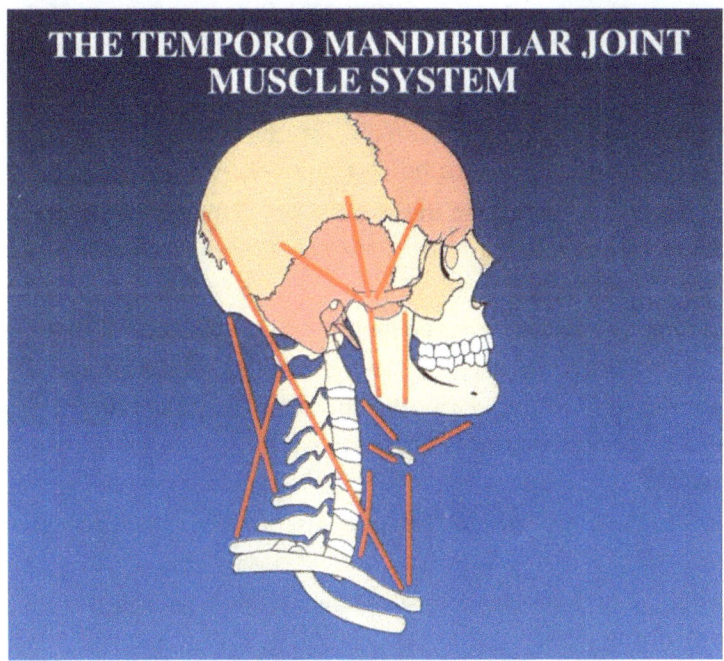

The muscle connections that maintain the relationship between mandible and skull (reproduced from Howat, 1999)

The importance of *reasonable* TMJ symmetry

These tests are a way to increase awareness of the movement of your own mandible. In most cases the asymmetry in the joint will be very slight and we are all slightly asymmetrical for the reasons already given. But because the mandible contains the lower teeth, which must meet the upper teeth on closure, it is important to regularly check. Pressing the sensitive forefinger on the joint space can expose minor joint disturbances that would normally go unnoticed. Movement of the mandible shares muscles with breathing, speech, singing and swallowing. It is the biggest and heaviest suspension of the head/neck area and its weight always encourages the head to nod downwards onto the chest. Small muscles at the back of the skull prevent this by always maintaining the balancing of the head on the occipital joint. It is also supported by a good tongue resting position which counterbalances the weight of the mandible- the mandible suspended down and forward, the tongue suspended down and back.

How the mandible moves

The mandible is a three way joint, which requires a complex system of muscles and ligaments to move it. The next diagram illustrates only the position and direction of movement of the capsular disc, as this is fundamental to the efficient co-ordination of all other movers.

The mandible is suspended in this housing by the action of muscles and ligaments, many of which also act upon the suspensory mechanism of the voice.

There are three stages to opening the mouth (see diagram on following page):

- The impulse to open the mouth contracts the lateral Pterygoid muscle, which originates in a bone that makes up the exterior part of the eye socket.
- This muscle inserts into the capsular disc, which slides forward with the contraction
- The mandible then slides forward and down following the contour of the skull
- Bear in mind that in efficient translation this will not be felt as a three-stage movement, but merely a glide of the jaw away from the skull.

This 'down and forward action' of the mandible as it moves away from the skull is called 'translation'. It provides a cushioned ride for the condyle of the mandible and prevents wear between the two joint surfaces.

It is important the jaw achieves maximum translation at the joint to provide maximum space for

- the airway from the nasal sinuses to larynx,
- swallowing,
- articulation and resonance of speech sounds,
- backwards and upwards movement of the front third of the tongue.

Functional movement of the mandible has close association with the functional activity of the pharynx, larynx, and with the skeletal muscle system of the neck (Kawamura, 1968)

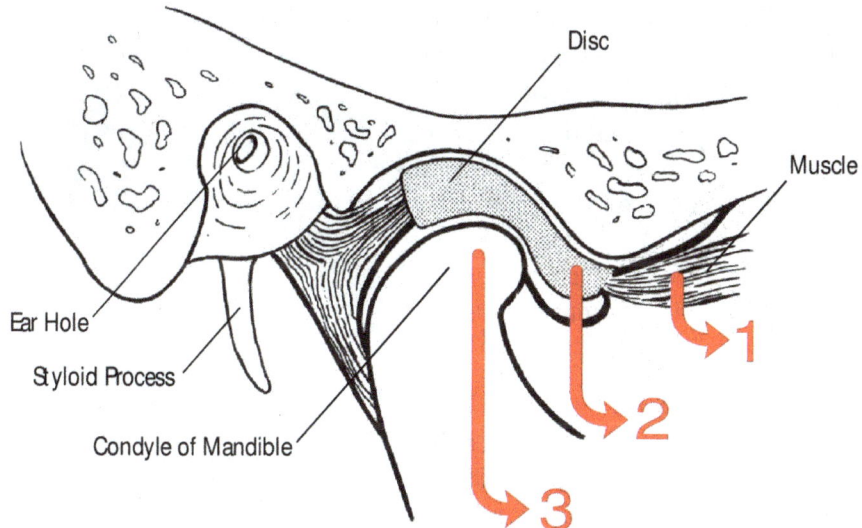

The 3-stage movement of the capsular disc of the TMJ (after McDevitt 1989)

What is happening when this joint clicks?
- Excessive clenching or grinding of the teeth.
- Multiple extractions of molar teeth have reduced the joint space and compressed the disk. This is turn causes ….
- Retraction of the mandible.

All of these and other causes drive the condyle further into the joint and limit joint space. The disc may become compressed and not glide as easily as it should. It may even stick so that the mandible travels some way without it. Eventually the disc will move all at once, with a resounding 'click'. This is the click you may feel under your fingers.

You can open your mouth and hinge at the joint by pulling the mandible down with muscles under the chin. The effect is to lengthen the face and lose expression from the eyes (see photograph illustrating tension in the chin).

Wherever breathing, face muscles, voice, and balanced posture are efficient and co-ordinated there will be even and efficient translation of the mandible in and out of the joint space. Conversely, a freely and efficiently translating mandible is a fair indication that the whole suspension of tongue, hyoid bone and larynx is well balanced and the body has reasonable symmetry.

Face, mandible voice

If you turn back to the universal perception of a beautiful face in Chapter 7 and then look at the pictures of faces with a translating mandible you will see that the translating mandible is also associated with the 'wider than long' face.

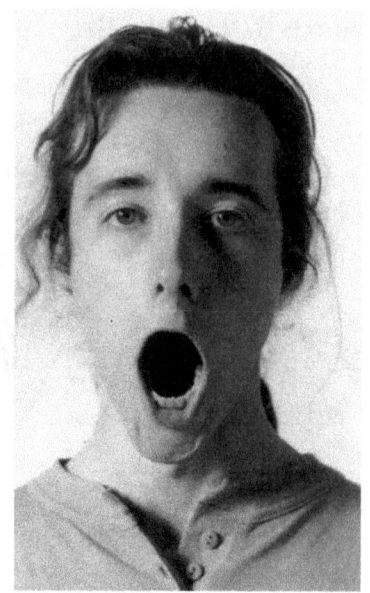
More hinging than translating

The mandible is viewed as a dental area because it houses the teeth, but only dentists and orthodontists who have taken the step beyond 'drilling, filling and billing' will concern themselves about the state of your TMJ and how it functions. A dentist concerned only with your teeth will record only one statistic: "How far does the mouth open?" This will be measured by the front opening like the one above. If you can hinge your jaw into the acceptable opening measurement, it can click and grind and feel really uncomfortable. But it must be OK because you can force it to a good opening at the front.

Howard Keel in 'Kiss me, Kate'

Richard Burton in 'Camelot'

Most muscle activity in the upper face, even looking down

Good use of face muscles dilates the nostrils to pull in air efficiently

This does not help the wind player (the singer is a wind player), the footballer, the skater, the mountain climber, because everything important for these activities relies on the TMJ translating. This opens the back teeth as well as the front teeth.

Beckham

Williams

All the faces on this page have strong muscle build across the upper part of the face: the skin around the eyes is stretched upwards and outwards, widening and opening the eyes. Translating jaws are not exclusive to actors and singers. Even without the smile, the efficient sportsman displays strong muscle action across the level of the eyes. See the photographs at the bottom of the previous page.

Is the secret of good translation of the mandible merely a broad smile?

No, not <u>quite</u> just a broad smile. The Temporalis muscle, usually snapping the teeth together to chew, has an additional role in the translation of the mandible. It is important to know that only the anterior section of Temporalis is involved and not the whole muscle as total involvement would have the opposite effect and snap the jaws together.

A few fibres of Temporalis blend with the fibres of that part of lateral Pterygoid, which glides the capsular disc forward. As the lateral Pterygoid contracts, so does the anterior part of Temporalis. This presents itself on the face as a widening across the region of the eyes, stretching the skin out and up – the direction of the fibres of Temporalis.

The difference between this and a smile is subtle and being encouraged to smile may access the correct muscle system. However, if you are paying

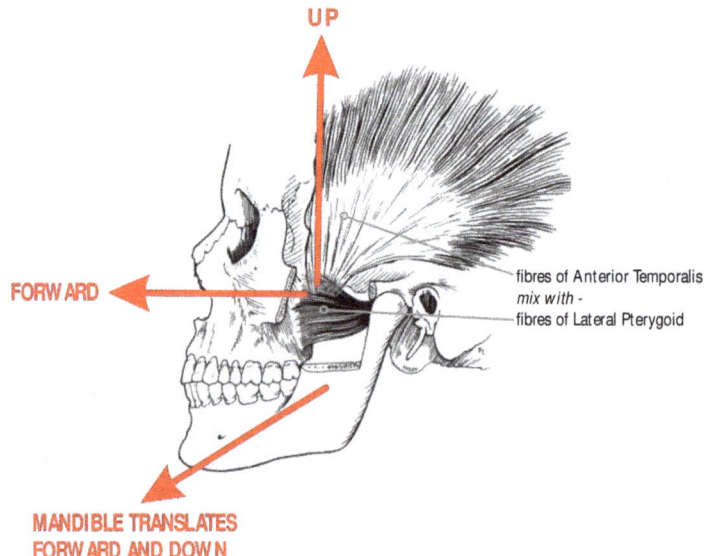

The 'forward and up' in translation of the mandible (after McDevitt, 1989)

the mortgage with the instrument you play, this is not enough. You have to know *exactly* what you are doing.

Lateral Pterygoid moves the mandible forward while Temporalis stabilizes this movement from above. It is interesting that Alexander recognised the directions of 'forward and up' for the head in relation to action of the body in any plane of movement. The jaw has to also have a 'forward and up' direction from the face muscles (lateral Pterygoid is a deep muscle of the face) in order to move efficiently through its three planes.

Experiment

Place your fingers on your cheekbones and walk them away from your nose until they arrive at your eye socket. Dig your middle finger in here in the spot that feels most tender. Keep this reference and use your first fingers to locate your jaw joint as you move your jaw side to side. Between these two fingers is the area where the front fibres of the Temporalis muscle come down from the temporal bone to mix with the fibres of the lateral Pterygoid muscle.

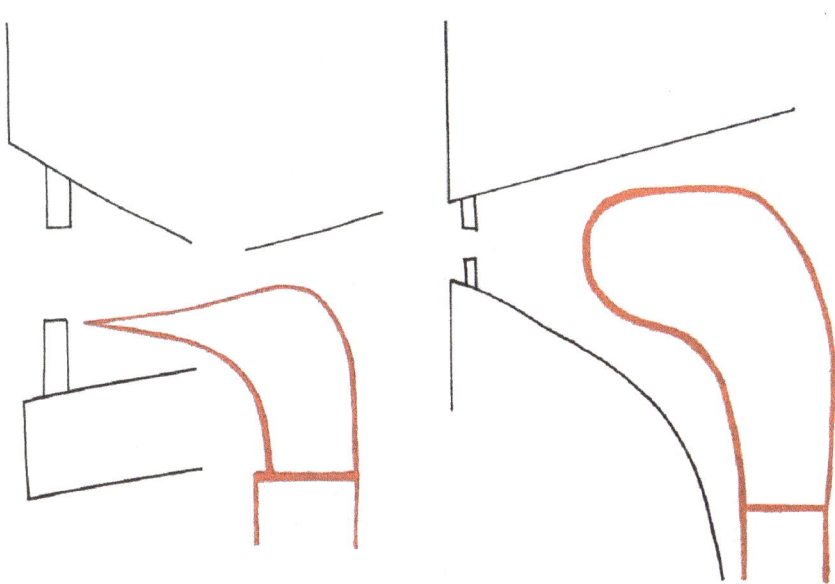

Limited translation of the mandible restricts tongue articulation

Free translation of the mandible assists tongue articulation

Keeping both references with your fingers, use your imagination to locate your upper lip and raise it. Think of the lateral face muscles and stretch your face upwards and backwards in the same way that you stretched the tongue upwards and backwards in order to click against the palate. You are now co-ordinating the work of anterior Temporalis and the lateral Pterygoid. If you still have a finger left put it behind your lower teeth and you will discover that your jaw has moved forward and down and your lower teeth are in front of your upper teeth.

The one activity common to most people that seems to automatically and almost reflexly translate the jaw forward and down is putting a toothbrush between the teeth to clean them. Try singing and brushing your teeth at the same time. This re-programmes the movers of face and mandible and co-ordinates lateral Pterygoid and Temporalis *very simply*. You will dribble a lot but don't worry about that.

There is no way that you can breathe, speak or sing efficiently without the full co-operation from movers of the mandible because:

- The weight and movement of the mandible has a direct effect on the position of the head on the spine;
- Asymmetry in the translation of the mandible will, in the long term, become a relative asymmetry in the suspension of the hyoid bone, affecting the downward movement of the larynx;
- Dysfunction of the TMJ, either from torsion of the temporal bones or from underdevelopment of the maxilla (see 'Teeth') will reposition the mandible and consequently the hyoid bone and all its suspensory mechanism.

The instructions -

- "Open your mouth more"
- "Drop your Jaw"

are likely to do more harm than good unless the person instructed already knows how to access the muscle system that brings this about and the relevance to that action on balance and posture.

Those who tell you to smile when you sing are helping you to access more efficient translation of the mandible, but it is not enough that you smile, it improves the sound of your voice, but you do not know why. You must understand the functional anatomy of it. Understanding is the one essential control system you need for your voice

Movement

Think about your tongue and its role in jaw movement. It is attached to both mandible and hyoid, so go back and reread in Chapter 6, The Importance of Tongue Position - how natural tongue posture helps to maintain the stability of the large heavy mandible from below. There is much activity in the area of the head and neck.

A Rough Guide to help you with your own moving model

When you are Chewing

1. The mandible is the prime mover
2. The tongue falls into the floor of the mouth to push food between the teeth (the only time it is there)
3. The larynx responds to the swallowing action of the tongue by closing the airway with the epiglottis

When you are Speaking or singing

1. The larynx produces the formant (basic pitched sound)
2. The tongue moves back and up to shape the vowels in the pharynx,
3. The mandible moves in response to the movement of the tongue.

This is arguably the most important information for the professional voice, as the jaw is actively either aiding or interfering with both articulation and breathing every time the mouth is opened.

Draw some diagrams of the tongue, mandible hyoid and their relative positions. Mark the styloid process of the skull and the ear hole. Put in some important muscles mentioned in the chapters on face, mandible, tongue and Jaws and teeth.

This could be the moment to buy a decent, clear, up to date anatomy book. None is recommended in the bibliography because they are being updated and improved all the time. Go for something simple and clear with good colour illustrations and try to get one that opens flat.

The Teeth

The mandible and the maxilla are designed to house 32 teeth, each tooth jointed into the bone. Joints contain sensory feedback systems – proprioceptors – and the concentration of sensory feedback in the dental area is such that it is quite impossible to enjoy one more moment of life with a raspberry pip somewhere in your teeth. You just have to get it out. This indicates the distress that can be caused through discomfort in the dental area.

The 32 teeth occlude, that is the arch of 16 teeth in the maxilla meets and integrates with the arch of 16 in the mandible.

"Every tooth in a man's head is as valuable to him as a diamond":
Cervantes, 1605.

The four front incisors are cutting teeth and the 5 premolars and molars are to grind up the food.

Get a mirror and examine your teeth. Identify each one and how many you have of the full set.

The position and size of the mandible is influenced by the development of the teeth. By meeting together in an even occlusion, the teeth guide the two condyles symmetrically into the TMJ. The teeth – how they develop, how many you retain, and for how much of your life, are a major influence on postural symmetry, not only of the jaw and the voice suspension, but also of the whole body and all of its functions.

Children's teeth

All of the dental literature now agrees that the best start for a lifetime of easy jaw, face and dental development is to be breastfed. The suckling action naturally forms a well-shaped palate by making the baby work hard to milk the breast. The tongue pulls back hard against the palate to pull at the nipple, unlike the action of sucking through a straw, in which the tongue comes forward to suck. The early sucking action begins the expansion of the palate and stimulates the eruption of the first teeth. When a baby has not been breastfed it is important to watch the development of tongue position and help this with lots of singing and smiling, first to the baby and then later, with the infant copying.

In the early developmental years, before the age of six, first teeth and the tongue are preparing the two dental arches for the eventual eruption of the much larger adult teeth. These arches need as much expansion as possible if the adult teeth are not to crowd and move out of line. Crooked teeth do not meet in an even occlusion and this can compromise the free translation of the jaw at the TMJ (see Chapter 3 for the activities that help develop this).

Speech is a major arch developer, followed closely by running, jumping, singing, and smiling. Children who have dummies/soothers/pacifiers in their mouths after they have achieved upright posture may retain a forward position of the tongue and develop speech problems. They also talk *less* and may not develop good broad arches with space for all of the teeth. Balance on two feet is compromised in these children by the body weight being thrown forward by the forward tongue.

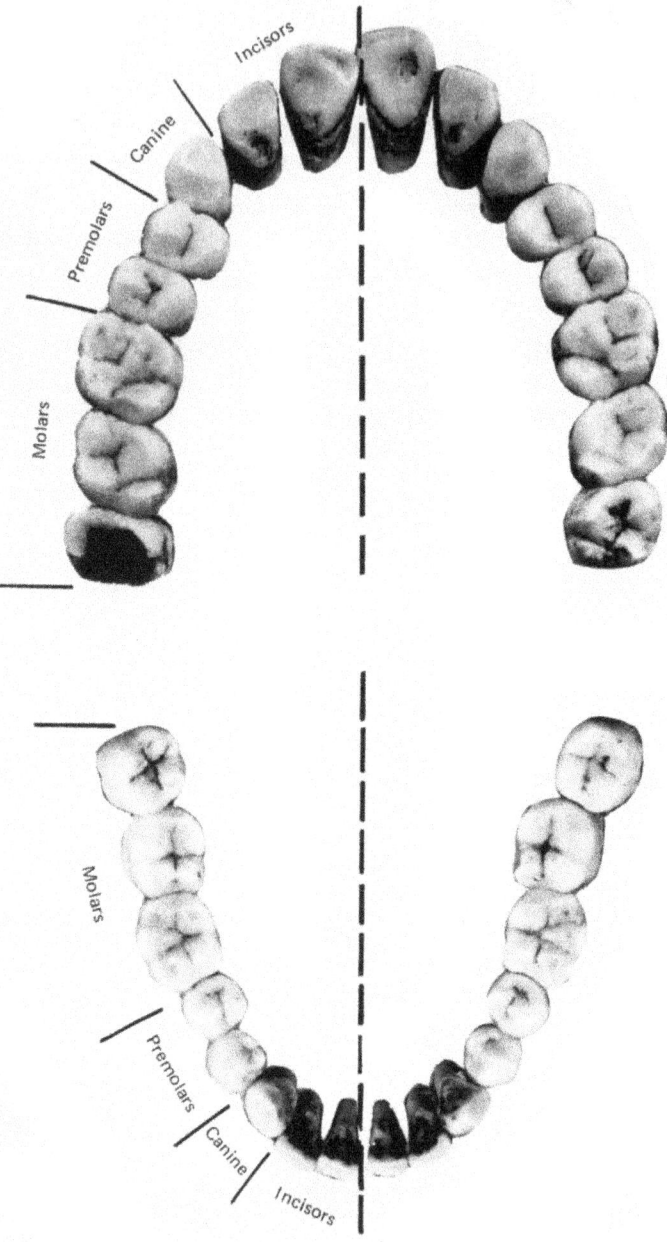

The complete adult dental arches with all 32 teeth
(reproduced from Hiatt and Gartner, 1987)

The jaw, the dental arches, the teeth, the face muscles, posture, breathing and speech all develop interdependently in these early years. Parents and schoolteachers should ideally monitor balance, posture, voice, teeth and arch development and discuss them. Then, before development is seriously affected activities and singing games can be introduced to promote extra activity in the weak area (see *Early VoiceGym*).

- A child not encouraged to talk and to sing will not develop full arch width.
- A child who is reluctant to engage in physical activities may have a restricted airway and inefficient breathing due to lack of development in facial muscles, or a narrow dental arch.
- A child, who constantly sucks fingers or thumb, will drive the jaw backwards into the joint and eventually displace developing teeth.
- A child not checked for cranial torsion in infancy may suffer underdevelopment of dental arches from minor birth trauma.

An annual check-up with a cranial clinician ensures development of stable physical patterns and may well prevent asthma and glue ear by opening up a restricted airway and as a result, the Eustachian tube.

In his book 'Your Jaws, Your Life', David Page says, "When a mouth is too small, early action should be taken to increase space for the teeth and for the tongue. By the age of six 80% of jaw growth has occurred. Traditional orthodontics often waits to diagnose at the age of 7 and treat at age 8-12. Active Functional jaw Orthopaedics treatment at age 2-6 can more successfully influence tooth, jaw and airway growth" (Page, 2003).

What is 'Functional Jaw Orthopaedics, or 'functional orthodontics'?

There are two ways to deal with all problems. One is to wait until the problem presents itself and then apply treatment already proven to solve that specific problem: this is how orthodox orthodontics operates.

Advantages

This is cost effective in the short term. The appearance of a problem sets the appropriate wheels (already oiled) in motion. Training of clinicians is also cost effective in the short term as diagnosis can be systematic and standardised.

Disadvantages

The problem presents itself because all means of compensating for it have been exhausted and the body is compromised. The presented problem will therefore be, potentially, one of many. Other problems are merely further down the exposure queue. In the long term these will also emerge and the cost of dealing with them will spiral.

Training for the recognition and treatment of specific problems in a systematic way does not encourage the questioning of the broader implications of that treatment. Neither does it encourage lateral thinking that may solve the problem another way

The other way to deal with a problem is to make sure you see it coming and prevent the problem happening at all by early intervention. This will be the policy of any orthodontist who practices functional jaw orthopaedics, or functional orthodontics.

Advantages of early orthodontics

Not only is the problem itself 'nipped in the bud', so are all the accompanying compensations for this developing problem. The child can develop individual skills without the feeling, both physical and personal, that 'something is always holding me back'. That 'something' may be the adverse effect that a narrow maxilla has on the breathing system.

No teeth are removed because the policy is to expand the bone structure to house all the adult teeth. The skeletal frame, which includes the full set of teeth, will remain intact. The adult voice will then respond fully to the physical, musical or language training necessary to attain a professional level of vocal efficiency.

Disadvantages

The young child will probably have to wear a light-wire functional dental appliance called an 'ALF'. However, the young child can cope with this so much more easily in real terms than the 12-14 year old, who is dealing with puberty and with all that puberty entails – peer pressure, sexual awareness, vocal rebalancing, educational pressure and much more.

Functional orthodontics is more costly in the short term, especially if you take a 4-6 year old for treatment. It is usual to charge more for adults than children in zoos, at eating places, the Tower of London, etc. The idea that the treatment of children should cost the same as the treatment of adults may demand a cultural rethink but in the long term functional orthodontics, like the early check by a cranial clinician for the presence of a strong cranial rhythm, will open developmental doors into life skills which cancel costs later in life because problems have been avoided by preventative treatment. This, in the long term, saves money, but much, much more than that. It rescues the development of potential

It saves the child from believing he can only come second or third when he could easily, on the commitment he makes, come first. However, his airway does not provide the space to cope with the extra efficiency required as he grows bigger and his breathing tank – the maxilla – becomes proportionally smaller.

It saves that 14 year old girl from the fixed 'tram tracks', With functional orthodontics when she is little, by the time she is 14 she will have a beautiful smile in a complete arch of teeth .The clinician who fixes tram tracks seems to have forgotten what it is like to be 14.

"I'm told I will have these 'tram tracks' on for at least a year. If I hold my face in this position I can cope with my peer group. The orthodontist made me count from one to twenty and said, "There you are, you can talk perfectly well, you'll be all right". I came out and went home and started hurting. I have some wax to put on but I hate eating – the food sticks to the metal. It hurts all the time and sometimes when I open my mouth the skin on the inside of my cheek gets caught on the metal and I could scream with the pain of that. But I am in class and I cry inside instead".

The age of the beginning of mixed dentition – approximately 6 years old - coincides with the arrival of the larynx at the end of its 'shift', (see Chapter1 – Early Development) and with the maturation of the central nervous system. By this age, about 90% of head growth and about 80% of jaw growth has already occurred (Facial Growth and Facial Orthopaedics – 1986). Crowded teeth, which require orthodontic intervention in early teens, begin at this early age with underdevelopment of the maxilla – the bone that houses the upper arch of teeth. This is when preventative measures could be taken, both in exercise, singing and in arch expansion.

As growth and independence increase opportunity –
1. Physical exercise, playing music, dance, singing and playing sport increase the development of balance and posture.

2. Good balance and posture encourage symmetry in the muscles of jaw and tongue.
3. This, in turn, encourages even and symmetrical development of the teeth. A well functioning breathing system provides the right equipment for the enjoyment of physical activity.
4. The physical activity, in turn, makes the demand on the other developing systems and encourages growth patterns.

This is a good cycle of growth and development. The person who regularly exercises all through life is more likely to develop and retain a well shaped facial bone structure with teeth that relate comfortably to each other and a jaw that does not interfere with breathing or voice

Early Prevention

If children are checked at age 4 or 5 by a dentist who practices *preventative* dentistry, under-development of the dental arches can be diagnosed and light wire removable appliances called Applied Light Function (ALF) can be fitted to expand the arch when it is at its most plastic. These appliances work very quickly, so treatment time is minimal and Early *VoiceGym* will reprogramme face muscles to continue making space for the teeth after treatment. The result is that all teeth erupt naturally and have the space to grow into an even arch.

The effect on Voice of Orthodox orthodontic procedures for crowded teeth

In 1996 I noticed that some of the singers I taught who were in late teens or early twenties hit a ceiling with their voices and musicianship that could not be explained. It is easy to make judgements of work or performance that blame the individual for lack of commitment, or easier still to judge that this person 'just hasn't got it' and has developed their skill as far as it can go. In many of these cases that did not make any sense to me since progress so far indicated that this singer had special ability. I began to ask questions about development outside music and singing and discovered that each of these singers had had standard orthodontic treatment for crowding that involved extracting teeth and wearing appliances, either removable or fixed, to reposition teeth earlier in their teens. If this had involved merely two or three singers of between 18 and 21 I would probably not have followed it up, but when I broadened the age range I began to discover that a large percentage of the population have had a similar orthodontic procedure in their early teens. I wanted to know whether this had an effect on voices or musical skills.

I decided to do a pilot study of ten singers who had experienced orthodox orthodontic treatment and plot their musical progress after treatment.

Removal of premolars for over crowded teeth

When the full set of adult teeth erupt, the dental arches need to have developed enough space for 32 teeth to sit evenly side by side. When there is not room for all the adult teeth and they crowd, the standard orthodontic procedure is to remove teeth *when the crowding has pushed other teeth out of line*. This is usually self evident by age ten or eleven, but standard orthodontic procedure is to leave the correction until about 13 or 14, when the teeth have finished major eruption.

The teeth removed are usually premolars – the 4s, see the diagram in this chapter of the dental arches. (Count the two central teeth as 1 and count out from there). Uppers or lowers can be removed, depending upon the personal configuration. In severely crowded cases all four premolars are removed. Apart from the consideration of loss of healthy teeth, which form part of the body's important proprioceptive feedback system, the arch is still underdeveloped and the teeth now have to be moved into an aesthetic position with permanent retaining tracks. These may be in place for one to two years.

This is the moment to revisit the information on Cranial Rhythm in Chapter 1 – Early Development. These braces to move the teeth cross the midline of the roof of the mouth (maxilla) and interfere with the rhythmic movement of the cranial bones.

The tram tracks and wire fitted to the teeth gradually close the gaps where teeth have been removed At the end of dental treatment the upper arch may be too narrow for natural tongue resting position, the tongue falling into the floor of the mouth because it does not fit into the narrow palate shape. A narrow, high arched palate restricts the airway and reduces the resting length of muscles of the soft palate and throat (pharynx).

Next time you watch competitive athletics, notice the faces of the winners. All have wide faces that indicate a wide upper arch to the mouth.

All display a wide arch of large, even teeth. The same is true of all people whose skills require efficiency in posture, breathing or voice.

Narrow arches and voice problems

My pilot study confirmed that in ten singers of an age range from 18 to 60, all of whom had had major extractions, there was a history of voice problems including intermittent voice loss, pitch problems, frequent throat problems as in tonsillitis or hoarseness, and in three cases, complete loss of the ability to sing. In one case, the desire to sing resulted in reverse orthodontics (Caine 1998).

Case History

A tenor of 18 years old had also been a promising tennis player and skier. It is not unusual to find that those who can play music well are also good at sport. Both require a high degree of co-ordination. At 17 he appeared to have a promising career in Music Theatre, having been selected to appear for two seasons in leading roles in National Youth Music Theatre productions and at the beginning of the second season he had made up his mind to audition for a Music College to study singing and pursue a career in music. Throughout that season of productions he experienced repeated voice loss, so that he could not be risked in a leading role. By the time the college auditions came he could not sing at all. His jaw would not open very far and the sound of the voice was awful. He auditioned for a University Music Department on the double bass, which he had always played well, in the hope that a teacher in the department would be able to help his voice.

I was teaching singing there at the time and he became one of the people on my pilot study, even though his instrument was now officially the double bass. First it had to be established that he did not have anything wrong with his voice itself. This may seem paradoxical- he had something *very* wrong with his voice, it did not operate at all but as you have discovered in the preceding chapters the voice is not just the mechanism that vibrates inside the larynx, it involves the whole body and brain. Tests revealed no pathology in the voice and the problem was medically diagnosed as 'stress'.

Premolars had been removed in his early teens and braces fitted to straighten the teeth. The whole facial complex was underdeveloped. His balance was really poor and he always fell off the balance board to the same side. This a fair indication of excessive torsion in the double spiral muscle system – the body pulls round to the left or right. This was substantiated by the serious tumbles he had experienced when practicing quick turns on skis. He could easily turn one way and always fell when turning in the opposite direction. His tennis game had received advanced coaching but he could no longer move quickly enough to cover the whole court.

Sport and music both demand time, commitment and precise levels of co-ordination. They are also activities of constant competition and stakes are very high. If children display early ability in sport or music, have the commitment, spend the time, falling standards must be symptomatic of something else.

My experience as a teacher indicates that no one who has enjoyed being good at something and the status it brings, gives up that feeling easily. This young tenor was growing and taking on more activities requiring precise co-ordination. The larger bone structure needed a more powerful breathing system, but the area of his face was not growing and had not been growing for some time. This was the cause of the crowded teeth, a symptom of lack of development. The facial bone structure would definitely not grow any more after the appliances were fitted on the *outside* of his teeth, pulling the teeth inwards to straighten them in a space now two teeth smaller in each arch. His dental arch was now too small for his overall size. See the first photograph, which was taken before work was begun to reverse the orthodontic treatment and give him back the space to breathe and sing.

There was another problem to correct. The tongue was forward and lying in the floor of the mouth. It, too, had grown and now no longer fitted into the roof of this small arch. To hide the appliances at the self-conscious age of thirteen, he had kept his mouth tight shut, holding lip muscles and masseter muscles (see Chapter 7- Face muscles). This effectively drove his jaw back into the TMJ. The development of the masseter muscles gave him, by 18 years old, the appearance of a chipmunk.

The tenor voice had emerged at 15-16 and he began to sing. I never heard this voice, only meeting him when the voice had completely failed, but it was obviously good enough to get him into National Youth Music Theatre. Now, at 18,

- The jaw was restricted, it hinged open, and it did not translate
- The tongue was forward and down
- The body was in asymmetrical torsion
- He could not sing at all

At 18, dental arch reduced by extraction of premolars

Functional orthodontics expanded the dental arches and replaced teeth, now a professional tenor

- The only physical symptom was jaw tension on one side of his face

He went away to think, while a dentist, a cranial chiropractor and myself sat down and considered the problem. The narrow maxilla had to be expanded in all directions if the voice were to develop further.

Whatever presented as a result of that would undoubtedly involve all of us.

Balance, posture, position of the mandible and position of the hyoid all had to change if he wanted to sing. The original orthodontics that had fixed his maxilla in a dimension that limited his breathing system, his body chemistry and consequently everything he wanted to achieve in life, needed to be reversed.

This was put to him and without hesitation he decided to take this on. Here are the before and after pictures of this tenor, who has now, seven years on, established a successful career as a professional tenor.

Physiological Adaptive Range

When you get to the last few yards of the race and suddenly run faster than you ever have before, or balance on one foot and stretch just one more inch beyond your reach for the jar on the top shelf you are pulling in the effort of muscles that were never designed to do this job. These are moments when you surprise yourself and go beyond the normal range of your ability.

These moments are exciting because they give you a real kick, strengthen your confidence, and encourage you to have an increased awareness of what you might achieve. Even simple, non-competitive events like reaching for something and managing that extra inch can do that for you. The human creature has a curiosity and a desire to push barriers and the body compensates for this by co-opting extra effort from surrounding muscle systems. On such occasions we step out of our normal physiological adaptive range.

This system is not only available for achievement and development of potential. It pulls us out of danger and provides a support system when our normal muscle system sustains injury or develops weakness. It can be termed 'extra money in the bank'.

During that long drive home at the end of the day shoulders may fall forward and you may lean on the steering wheel. Compensatory muscle systems support this poor posture and you do not collapse, but the effort is taking its toll, because you are using more and more compensation the longer you drive like that. Sooner or later the brain recognises that the compensation is becoming the norm and the system becomes programmed as 'general use'. You are no longer temporarily compensating. You have now adapted the system and the adaptation will be used as the normal day-to-day system.

You have now used up a chunk of your physiological adaptive range. It has ceased to be adaptive. You are draining your capitol. You are draining away the body's physical bank account and it is not a bottomless pit. Like running out of money, running out of adaptive range is likely to bring you to a painful full stop. These are the times we become ill, or we injure ourselves. They are times when the organism cannot cope. We have exceeded physiological adaptive range. Illness may not always be physical – end of range can lead to emotional or psychological stress, it can manifest itself during moving house or moving jobs. We deal with the financial situation by putting money back into the bank. Similarly exercise and understanding allow you to recover natural voice, body and brain patterns if you keep learning and questioning established practice. This restores Adaptive Range to within its limits.

Ageing and dentition

Loss of teeth with age is inevitable but where possible crowns and implants maintain contact with the bone structure in a way that dental plates never can. This is not in everyone's financial possibilities so. When you wear dental plates, don't remove them at night, or anytime except to clean them. You are removing part of the support system for your ageing skeletal structure. You need as much help as you can get!

Dental Distress

The loss of teeth, poor occlusion and misalignment of the TMJ are all major stressors that affect adaptive range. If you sing, play a musical instrument, run and play contact sports, and if co-ordination and skill are deteriorating, it could be that your jaws and teeth are telling you something. Listen to them rather than friends who tell you that you are over the hill.

Teeth wear down with age, but the process is so slow and so gradual that it generally goes unnoticed. It is another of those dental areas that your dentist may never mention but if you grind your teeth (brux), chew your nails, bite the inside of your mouth, etc. wear will accelerate and you will lose 'vertical' height. This is the distance from the TMJ to the back corner of the jaw. This measurement is dependant on the height of the molars and whether you retain them. Breathing loses efficiency with loss of vertical height and the head, shoulders and tongue are driven forward. See Fonder's model in Chapter 1. for the effect of occlusion on the head and shoulders.

Functional orthodontists will treat adults who realise that the folly of their early dental treatment is presenting current problems. Anyone who plays an instrument should have regular checks on occlusion of teeth and TMJ function. See Useful Contacts at the end of the book for dentists who are aware of the links between physical efficiency, the state of the dentition and performance.

10. Words and Rhythm

Beginnings of Language

If you were dropped into the jungle to listen to the noises of the animals you would hear all the pitch the human voice can make. You would be deafened by a cacophony of vocal sound swooping up to the highest pitch the human can achieve and down to the lowest. The loudest and the quietist would be there - the screech, growl, and moan. The noises made by the primates swinging through the trees would be closest to our human sound, any singer would envy the ease with which the pitch soars and swings. But this cacophony lacks the regular pattern of rhythm and pitch that would turn these random swoops into human speech and song.

Speech would enable us to define our past and our future and encourage us to think of the continuity of our existence. It would allow us to make ethical judgments and be a means of memory and introspection. It would allow us to express ourselves in song with a human voice and this would lead to the playing of instruments, music and dance. The sophisticated patterns of rhythm and pitch that developed out of a need to communicate the new thinking patterns would provide a structure for both speech and music.

Most animals can communicate with sound: the mammals have very highly developed vocal communication patterns...yet no other animal had developed speech. We might marvel at the whales and the dolphins and their ability to 'talk' to one another; we may describe the chimp as being able to communicate on a human level by responding to specific questions and sounding requested vowels, no animal has yet voiced anything remotely comparable to "Earth hath not anything to show more fair" (Ode on Westminster Bridge, Wordsworth) Only a human has that measure of articulatory competence.

Where did speech suddenly come from?

It took two significant and singular evolutionary developments before sophisticated speech could emerge as the tool that would drive Homo sapiens forward far beyond the development of the other animals.

1. The enlargement of the frontal lobe of the brain

According to Crosby, Humphrey and Lauer (1962),"From developmental and phylogenetic standpoints, it is the differences in the frontal lobe that distinguish most especially the human from the subhuman brain".

Crelin (1987) stated, "I think it is quite reasonable to assume that the increase in size of the frontal lobes of the hominid brain during evolution reflect an increase in the ability to have a highly sophisticated language and conceptual or abstract thought".

2. The attainment of upright posture

Homo Sapiens are the only completely upright creatures. With upright posture and the subsequent rearrangement of the head/neck muscle system, the larynx achieved its lowest position yet. The tongue now formed a right angle with one third in the mouth and two thirds in the throat. The tongue could now spring backwards and it is this back spring that made the sounding of consonants mechanically possible.

Upright posture and the new tongue position facilitated not only the articulation of consonants but also many more vowels, enabling the sounding of a greater diversity of speech patterns. The uniquely skills of abstract reasoning and conceptual thought developed within the same time scale. It is not beyond belief that they developed each other. With time the co-ordination of walking, talking and thinking developed into repetitive patterns, or rhythms, which facilitated the planning and organizing of our lives. Language, song, dance and the playing of instruments were the result of co-coordinative development of upright posture, uniquely human conceptual thought and the rhythms of speech.

One individual personal growth and development is a mini version of the whole of evolution. All the different stages of our forefathers from the living cell, through amphibian, reptilian, mammalian stages and to the present upright creature are represented if we look at a single human developmental pattern from conception to the adult (Crelin 1976).

Between 100,000 and 500,000 years ago there was a gradual acquisition of a complex spoken language. It was not until 5,000 years ago that the first written language appeared. This pattern shows us that the best way to develop communication skills is through the ear and not the eye. Language is dependant on the ear and the development of the use of language in speech and singing needs to pre-empt the development of reading and writing, The ear and vestibular mechanism is present in utero, babies cannot focus the eyes when first born. Light and sound aid this focusing process during the first weeks of infancy. We can conclude from this that in language the ear is the leader and the eye follows. This is born out by the fact that we can close the eyes but never close down our hearing.

Language relies heavily on listening and allowing the ear to guide the voice through both the mental processing of words and the imagination (abstract reasoning and conceptual thought). Everyone speaks differently because everyone has a unique co-ordination of brain, voice and upright posture. Personal differences include voice pitch, resonance, and the efficiency and flexibility of the articulation system that converts voiced sound into intelligible sentences, but all language learning has to be 'voiced' before you can store it in your memory. When we hear ourselves read aloud or explain something it is through the ear – listening to ourselves - that we check our understanding of the information, our emotional and physical response to it, and our ability to apply previously acquired knowledge and life experience in this particular context. Voicing what we think opens up the possibility for access to the minds and experience of those who hear what we say. Listening to <u>ourselves</u> read or speak is vital for the passage of information into the inner brain centres of memory, understanding and wisdom.

Text became available to everyone in the Western World as a tool of the Reformation of the Church in the late fifteen hundreds, but most people could not read until education for all became a late nineteenth century drive, motivated by the increased wealth and urbanization resulting from the Industrial Revolution. Until then news, information and life experience was passed on by an oral tradition of storytelling and singing. Minstrels visited, you listened and then later, you retold the story. This oral tradition remains 'best practice' in the development of children's speech. Stories are told, events discussed and children listen, relating in turn, versions of the story for themselves.

For the last two hundred years, with the increased access to writing, reading and printing, the eye has become increasingly dominant in our perception of language. Now language is synonymous with text, even though text is visual and language dependent upon sound and the ear. Books are said to be 'in English' as opposed to 'in print'. This gives the wrong message about the relationship between text and language. It implies that they are the same. We 'read English' at University, meaning that we study the language, but mainly we study it through the eye dominated text. A teacher will ask a child to read a poem aloud from a book and it may never be pointed out to that child that everyone who has ever read that poem has seen the same thing in the book, but in the reading of it aloud the child will automatically make that poem unique and special to this moment.

The more emphasis we put on text, in education, in the workplace, in life, the more emphasis we put on the visual and allow understanding of the visual to be the whole process of learning and the less emphasis and exercise we give to the voice/ear relationship. Text does not in itself exercise the voice. You can read it and learn from it silently. You can communicate with the world all day using text messaging and never utter a sound: the term 'communication skills' has been redefined.

The voice is losing power fast. Every public hall is equipped with a sound system. No one gives a speech or a lecture now without amplification to assist what is referred to as 'projection'. A large chunk of the budget for any Musical Theatre Society, amateur or professional, is the sound system. No voice, however professionally trained, expects to operate without it. The answer to the horrendous voice problems experienced by the teaching profession leads me to predict that classrooms will inevitably also receive sound systems. It is only a matter of time. Do we let the voice go and concentrate on means of communication that develop computer skills, email, text- messaging?

Is the voice that important?

Maybe the voice is a transitory stage in the evolutionary process – a means to develop the shorthand we are all now using. Maybe the voice can now go and 'visual' is the next stage of dominance. Maybe text is all and a new creature is emerging.

If you accept the interdependence of upright posture, brain development and language development in Homo Sapiens, it would seem that to lose the continued development of language might also prove to be ultimately a reduction in physical and mental function. With this in mind I believe we should be exercising brain, voice and body all three together in order to develop all three together. It is my experience that this method of development achieves all round excellence in voice skills, ability to think laterally and on one's feet, and all round health and fitness. The alternative of separately learning singing, speech, sports and exercise, then attempting to learn exclusively through books has no parallels in evolutionary development where learning has always been experiential as well as via the intellect.

But the voice is not merely a means of communication. I have the advantage of knowing what it feels like to have a voice that does not really reflect your personality. My voice problems, which gave my voice a hard edge and made speech and singing an uncomfortable experience demonstrated graphically the frustration of hearing someone who isn't you selecting language that you would not choose to add your thoughts in general conversation. My worst difficulties were in presenting myself or my skills or when I attempted to console, listen to, or strongly support loved ones. My voice did not reflect the sympathy I felt and I was left with a feeling of inadequacy and loss. Even remembering those years invokes sadness.

Conversely the voice that is comfortable, powerful (not the same as loud) and comes from within carries with it such a feeling of satisfaction and well being, even when you are wrong. Being wrong with conviction is infinitely preferable... This voice is so much more supportive, loving, skilful and attractive to listen to. It also sings, which helps to develop the imagination and hence our entrepreneurial skills. How could we do without this quality in our lives and still have a life of quality? I will never cease to be grateful for having discovered the way to this..

The relationship between speech and singing

We are born singing. It is the primary function of the voice. The babbling and cooing noises of the baby are all singing, resembling the noises of primates. But then we are not yet upright and we have not developed all of our brain. When we are eventually on our feet we learn to speak through listening and copying voices and phrase patterns around us. Then, later still, someone else may complete the cycle by teaching us to sing songs developed in the language we now speak. Our primary vocal function of singing now includes rhythms of of speech and rhythms of music

Ideally a child passes through all of these stages before the age of approximately 6 years old. Within those first 6 years our voices are guided, developed, underdeveloped, driven, encouraged or discouraged onto a path that will probably be set for life. Parents are not given any information on how to guide this process and there is no training in voice for any teachers in schools, either to deal with their own voices or give out all this life developing instruction. A sobering thought. Sobering enough to encourage me to develop Early *VoiceGym* for this age group.

Case history

Ruth is 46. She had never been able to speak up for herself because although in her head she had many times wanted to, she knew that her voice would sound weak, breathy and all of fifteen years old when she did,. She had lost the connection between her speech and her singing. Some teacher, not necessarily a music teacher, but very likely, had told her not to sing with that 'awful voice', so she had never sung again. From that moment her voice lost its connection with play and fun, the range of pitch and colour in her speech became limited and she never used her voice more than was appropriate and necessary. She needed to go back and pick up that connection between speech and singing so I gave her the 'game' of reading children's stories aloud and singing every verb she came to. This 'talk-sing-talk-sing' gradually brought her singing and speech into the same voice and some loud, aggressive noises began to emerge that quite shocked her. She had never before given herself permission to let her voice break out of the control she felt she must maintain so that he voice did not sound 'awful' as the teacher had described it. This control had kept her voice in 'child mode', never allowing the adult voice to develop. She began to give herself permission to play with the sounds she discovered– where was the risk, doing this silly game? She used her singing to experiment with and get to know her emerging adult voice.   Her voice had finally grown up– at 46.

An interesting experiment

At your next party, ask everyone to write down the teachers they most remember and the subjects they enjoyed in school – maybe they became so interested in these subjects that they went on to study them in further education. Finally write down what they are now doing for a living, or what interests them most. Ask them about the voices of those teachers that inspired them. Discover whether there is any parallel between the good voices and the subjects in school people found interesting and worth pursuing.

What could o children teach us about language?

We are always so sure that children have to be taught, but there are some clues about the way words work that we can learn from them.

When they make up their own words they always emphasize the vowel:
- "ner–ner–ner–ner–ner" (absolute derision)
- "ba–ba–ba–ba–" (fire engine? Police car?)
- "ma-ma"
- "da-da"

and they don't put a consonant on the end!

They know instinctively that this weight of tongue and larynx must journey down the throat if their language skills are to progress, so single syllables, landing on the vowel and accompanied by banging the heels on the ground make up most of a one to two year old vocabulary. Lots of rhythmic singsong wordplay goes on, sometimes to someone, sometimes to no one. If only we would learn from this – it is the fundamental development of the mechanism we use for speech and most of the time we believe it is merely the gabbling of children who have not yet learnt to do it properly. Adults correct them. "Mu<u>mm</u>y" "Da<u>dd</u>y" "Ta<u>bl</u>e" emphasizing the consonants to correct the word.

Ultimately the voice must resonate in the chest – the largest empty space we have. Like all other instruments we need a sound-maker – in the case of

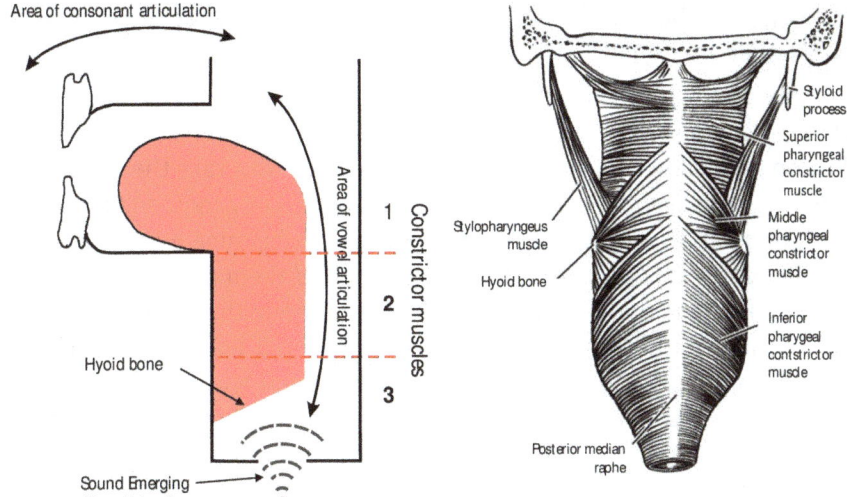

What happens inside the three constrictors (after Caine, 2003)

Use all three constrictors of the pharynx for articulating vowels (after Hiatt and Gartner, 1987)

the voice – the vocal folds within the larynx. We then need the sound produced in the larynx to rattle around in a large space and if possible set vibrating any surrounding structures, not to mention the bone conduction from the mass of the skeleton. There are lots of spaces in the breathing complex, the throat, the sinuses, the mouth – but nothing as large and empty as the chest and nothing with the potential for bone conduction like the ribs, spine, shoulder blades, shoulder girdle and front of the face.

The crucial bit of information that every child has and many adults have forgotten is that only the vowels have the potential for powerful and sustained resonance, which is why all children emphasize them. The voice is *all* vowel: the voice only does vowels. It does not do consonants. Other parts of us do the consonants: parts that are much higher up than the where the voice resonates in the chest.

Consonants are made in the mouth with lips and tongue slapping, exploding against hard palate, teeth, back of the pharynx.

Vowels are made much lower down and resonate even lower.

Do some vowels for yourself. Put your hand flat on the upper part of your chest and make a vowel last for the count of three or four. As you count in your head let the vowel bounce on the counts. If you swing your bum to the counting the vowel will resonate even harder in your chest. Feel the buzz under your hand.

Now do some consonants for yourself. What did you say? Pee? Ef? Gee? El? Or did you say Pu? Ku? Mu? None of these are consonants. They are all consonants followed by, or preceded by, a vowel. Now take the vowel away from the consonant and sound them once more. They shouldn't sound like explosions of air but the noises you might make bursting a crisp packet of tapping your nails on a window. You can *sound* them but you cannot *say* them unless you add a vowel. Muscles make them: the tongue, using the hard surface of the palate, and the lips. Occasionally lips, tongue and teeth come into contact. Do some, using only these areas and not the voice. You will discover that there is no sensation anywhere except in the mouth and the area surrounding. No sensation remotely connected with any bit of you below the chin.

Now you understand the difference between consonants and vowels ,look at the differences between text and language.

Text is
- only black and white,
- has spaces,
- is horizontal and every letter has equal importance,
- is dominated by consonants, not vowels (a ratio of roughly 2-1),
- lacks pitch, colour, expression, emotion, rhythm and gender,
- the same to everyone's eye.

Language is
- sound and colour,
- continuous,
- vertical – from the consonants occurring in the mouth you spring down to the vowels resonating in your chest,
- dominated by vowels, which can be sustained,
- variable in pitch, expression, emotion and gender, rhythm,
- different to everyone's ear.

At this point some readers must be jumping up and down about 'mmms', 'nnnns', lllls', etc. which fall into the category of voiced consonants. Mine is a practical approach. When you are voicing this 'mmm' and you open your lips you will produce a vowel. The same happens with all the other voiced consonants. They are really interrupted vowels. Maximum resonance and bone conduction on vowels is gained by minimum interruption from *all* consonants, voiced or unvoiced. My policy is therefore to treat all consonants the same way. Build tongue and lip muscle to articulate them fast and accurately. Keep them as short as possible, because they interrupt the down spring onto the vowel. You have only to hum a song on 'MMM' to feel the upward pull on the larynx.

When you hum on "NNNNN" with the mouth open and the tongue pulled back and up the larynx drops and you breathe through your nose. Try humming a nursery rhyme with your mouth open and your tongue pulled back and up.

Resonance and Bone Conduction

There is a great deal of emphasis placed on resonance and where it occurs in the disciplines of both speech and singing training. Singers and professional speakers are often confused by conflicting messages that encourage them to focus or 'place' the resonance of the voice into certain key areas and my experience is that those key areas are often the head and face. All other instruments are developed from the voice, so by looking at the resonance on musical sound as created by say, a cellist, a less confusing picture may emerge. The cellist bows the string and the vibration of that string, excited by the bow, makes the sound. The pitch is determined by the stopping of the string by the fingers of the left hand against what is interestingly called 'the neck' of the cello. The string where the sound is made is the nearest part of the instrument to the audience. From the string the sound goes, not towards the audience, but away from it and into the body of the cello, which is an empty box having a particular shape. We are shaped like a cello, or rather the cello is shaped like us and Mann Ray's photograph 'Le violin d'Ingres' demonstrates this beautifully.

So the sound springs away from the direction of playing and back towards the player to gather its resonance and so it is with the voice. The sound is made in the larynx which is in the throat and springs down into the large empty space of the cello shaped trunk to gather resonance from the cavern of the chest. The singer feels this resonance in various other places because the chest resonance is picked up by the flexible bone structure through which it passes to reach the audience. High, low, loud, soft sounds vibrate bones differently due to the different harmonic frequencies and the higher you sing the more those

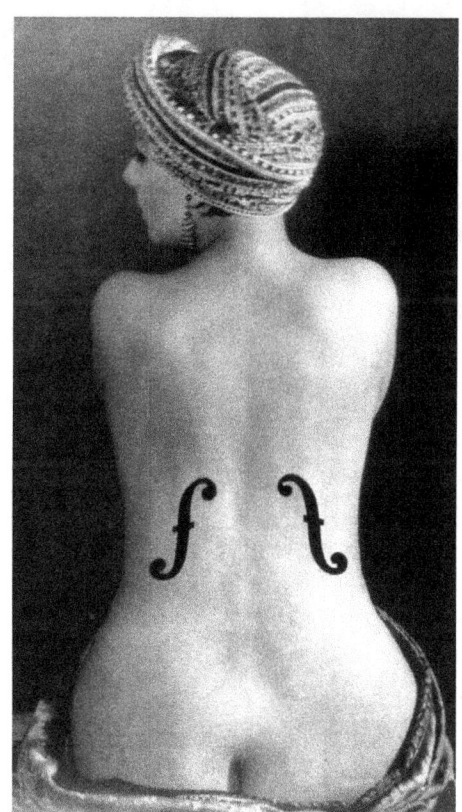

Le Violin d'Ingres (Man Ray, 1924)

small facial bones will rattle. To feel these different vibration sensations is good and an indication to the singer of the freedom of the voice, but to determine where the sound needs to be felt and attempt to direct it there is to reduce the down-spring of the larynx and the resonance in the whole voice. Resonance is in the chest, bone conduction can give you sensations almost anywhere there are small flexible bones. The skull is very mobile, particularly in the small facial bones. Hence sensation in the face is likely to be very strong when singing high, but the cause of that is always the down spring of the voice into the body.

Rhythm in your Speech

The rhythm of language can begin when the child moves on from single syllables to putting them together in short sentences. This begins with repetitive, or 'rote' rhythm, as is found in nursery rhymes. Children naturally speak like this in a da-de-da-de-da, kind of rhythmic pattern, although unlike nursery rhymes, they don't bother to rhyme the ends of lines. If you look at the rhythmic pattern of nursery rhymes many of them fall into a repetitive rote pattern.

Experiment

Say some nursery Rhymes and mark the rhythm. Clap it or click fingers. A tambourine is good.

Read Aloud

It is not the silent reading of books that develops articulate and communicative children, but articulate, talkative and singing adults. Simple rote rhythms in rhyme and song are vital throughout the first six years of life, when growth and maturation of the Central Nervous System (CNS) depends upon 'doing'. The larynx has not completed its downward shift before six years old and as early as 1947 it was noted that reading readiness seemed to coincide with the shedding of the milk teeth and that individual variation in the timing of the eruption of the second teeth might be indicative of other aspects of neurological maturity related to reading readiness (Ames1967).

Multi-syllabic words demand both light and heavy emphasis and rapid movement of throat, tongue and face muscles. That is turn requires strong and flexible movements of the vocal suspension. Muscular development in the upper body is the result of early establishment of balance and co-ordination. Sitting reading books does not develop the mechanics of language and communication. Children may learn lots of words this way, but they will not necessarily be able to communicate with those around them or demonstrate their own special skills – except in written examinations! See the Appendix for ideas for reading material.

Teaching Children to Read

This is the usual procedure -

It begins with the alphabet: "Ay, Bee, Cee, Dee, Ee, eF, Gee", etc

Then there is a second alphabet to learn: "A, Bu, Ku, Du, E, Fu", etc.

We are then told that "Bu, E, Du", spells 'BED'. Surely this spells 'BU-E-DU'?

You have already discovered that consonants and vowels are not mechanically the same, but this system convinces the child that they are!

If only language skills were kept ahead of reading skills and all children learned that a written word represented this or that combinations of sounds and pictures.... But text becomes dominant very early and thereafter can become 'what we read and understand' instead of the *nearest possible representation* of what we read and understand.

School is very busy and the main aim of reading is to be able to gain information and pass exams. Reading for its own sake and reading aloud ceases to have any purpose beyond the age of entry to secondary school and consequently the reading of rhythms that step outside the parameters of everyday speech are generally impossible for the average 15 year old. Muscles are not exercised and only very basic language rhythms have been observed for most of school life. Unless this 15 year old sings, or belongs to a home life where talking, debate, conversation and discussion are the norm, even the best law degree will not develop the skill for the court; the most skilled surgeon will not be able to reassure the patient.

Best Practice in Language Skills

The language we speak has regular rhythm patterns that we learn, programme, and then store. Flexibility depends upon constantly exercising different ways of expressing thoughts, emotions, problems and demands. In fact all the communication required for daily life. What one person can learn of language during the years of education and training cannot ever be enough to ensure that all events are covered. Like every other physical mechanism the voice has to be exercised. Like the rest of the body, the voice has to stretch, work out and extend beyond daily requirements.

Whatever language you speak, there is a heritage of writing available to you on which to exercise your voice in all facets of expression, emotion, rhythm and life experience. However reluctant you are to investigate what others have written, some of it will apply to you, you are probably not unique in your own culture. There is something very comforting in discovering that someone else felt exactly as you do, especially if it is 300 years ago that they felt it. You begin to realize there are no new problems to solve and there are answers for your particular one in somebody's book. Voicing those phrases, or verses, aloud puts you in touch with inner feelings that you may not be able to voice in your own terms. Other's words allow those feelings to be aired and maybe ultimately resolved.

Vowel priority in the voice, vowel resonance in the chest, connects voice and emotion. A voice resonating in the whole of the body is a voice resonating in the gut – the seat of emotion. There is no connection between consonants and emotion because they do not connect with gut resonance, or even with resonance at all. They are made in the mouth. Vowel emphasis, vowel priority is the key to emotion and expression in the voice, whether experienced by the speaker, or the audience. Both will feel the connection when the voice resonates inside the speaker.

Received Pronunciation

English is one of the few languages to have suffered from having a 'proper' version. Received pronunciation (RP) appears in the Military, separating the officers from the men; the Church, separating the upper and lower clergy; the Law, separating the lawyer from his clients; Medicine, separating the consultant from his patient; the Aristocracy, separating them from everyone else.

What is it?

In Received Pronunciation, <u>everything</u> in the text must be pronounced – 't' is exploded, 'r' is rrrrrolled and 'and' has a 'd', or even a 'du' on the end. Words that begin with a vowel must be separated from the word before.

A Roald Dahl poem would go like this in RP:

<u>A</u>ll those <u>O</u>ily boily bodies

<u>O</u>ozing <u>O</u>nwards <u>I</u>n the gloam

Each of the underlined capital letters would receive a kick form the throat, almost like a cough. It is called a 'glottal stop' and it kicks the larynx up instead of allowing the natural down spring that would emphasize the vowel. There is at least one word beginning with a vowel in every English sentence and the voice that uses this device eventually programmes a high larynx and vowels resonating only in the upper constrictor. The voice becomes consonant prioritised and the definition of individual words becomes more important than the continuous flow of phrases. Introducing this glottal stop effectively removes emotion from the voice, which no longer resonates in the deep throat spaces or the chest.

Where does it come from?

The Industrial revolution had thrown 'social class' into chaos. The aristocracy was losing money while the traders and manufacturers were making money. Dialect was also in chaos because people were moving into the cities to work and losing their roots. The new queen, Victoria, had married a German Prince, for whom structure and system were important. This enriched our culture in architecture and planning, but imposed a 'Queen's English', which dictated that all educated people were recognized by the way that they spoke. Schools taught RP in the teaching of reading, elocution was taught to introduce 'proper English' to those who wanted to better themselves educationally, socially. Whoever could afford it acquired it. RP ensured that people you met believed you were educated and it opened social doors closed to the northern or Birmingham accent. Even a late as the 1940s the BBC promoted RP by insisting that all its presenters spoke in this impersonal language. Regional accents emerged with the development of television and are slowly being valued once again for their colour and rich resonances. However, there is still some way to go.

Case History

Serina is Nigerian, big, black and beautiful. She is working here as a nurse and wanted to continue the singing lessons she had had in Nigeria, so that she could sing in a group and meet people. She belonged to a church and wanted to sing gospel and soul music. She sang for me. The voice was pale and ineffectual. She sang a hymn, sticking to the written vocal line, words carefully and singularly defined. I could not believe that this voice, which had only just come into this culture, sounded not black, but white – and ineffectually white at that.

I asked her to sing in her native language and the voice immediately and dramatically 'grew up'. The missionary school she went to in Nigeria was her passport to higher education, but it robbed her of her natural vocal inheritance because she was taught to speak and sing 'RP English' with a raised larynx. That was the way all the teachers in her school understood and spoke English so that was what she learned. Of course they did not speak her language, so there was no cross-fertilization.

RP was the English of colonialism. No one who speaks naturally speaks with a high larynx. The teaching of RP imposed a control on speech and breathing that affected the connections between the use of language and the right and left-brain. RP was an early Victorian concept, useful in controlling and schooling the native population that had to be governed by the English administration.

Voice Projection

This is an unfortunate descendant of RP that has not yet bit the dust. If you are emphasising consonants to 'project your voice' to the back of the hall/theatre concert hall, you are making consonants very important. But the voice does not *do* consonants. Return to the difference between text and language and reconsider. You need to talk to yourself. The cavity that enhances and enlarges the sound of the vowel - your chest - is not 'over there' but 'in here'. The vowel you sound rattles about inside you, sets up resonance, as in a cave, and flings it out in all directions while you remain talking and listening to yourself. Remember King Kong standing on the Empire State Building and beating his chest to show how powerful he was. You need to beat that sound in your chest to show how powerful *you* are. Your voice will then go wherever you want to send it and you will always be heard. You just need to look at the people you are talking to for the voice to have the focus of communication. When you look at them still talk or sing into yourself.

Here are some terms widely associated with voice that become confused when voice action is discussed, plus some points to clarify them.

Explosion – as in 'explode the consonants!'

Projection is based on Explosion: you explode the consonant in an attempt to project the vowel.

Received pronunciation encourages explosion of consonants

In 'Night and day' there are two pronunciations of 'd'. That is not the way people talk to each other. It is not language: It is text. We actually say 'Nightanday', or even 'nightnday'. The emphasis now lands on the two vowels in the two important words.

Silent reading of text encourages explosion

You *see* spaces between words. You *see* more consonants than vowels. You *see* horizontal lines of information with no rhythm; you *see* black and white, not colour.

Explosion – driving the voice forward to be heard – doesn't work

Projection is based on upspring, not down spring

It attempts to work against gravity, so it is effortful and, in the long term, ineffectual. It also encourages over breathing.

Voice resonance is based on <u>Implosion.</u> You implode consonants to achieve maximum down spring (resonance) on vowels

- Rhythm is dependant upon down spring followed by rebound. We are controlled by gravity, all rhythm works like this, whether you want to ice skate, throw a hammer, play tennis or play the violin. You punch gravity and use the rebound for sustaining power.
- Watch the conductor of the orchestra. He knows how rhythm works. '1' is always a downbeat of the baton.
- Rhythm is in the vowels. When you say "sea-witch" it is the 'ea' and 'i' that lands on the beat, not any of the consonants.
- Consonants are necessary and important to the understanding of sophisticated human language, but they are the beads and the embroidery on the fundamental structure. They have no gender, no emotion, and everyone's consonants sound the same. One utterance of one vowel can convey everything personal and felt

- Only conversation, reading aloud and poetry can give us rhythm in speech. Poetry more than anything else, because it opens up the possibilities for exploring rhythms outside our personal experience. If we bang the same drum with the same rhythmic message and have no relief from that people switch off. They are bored, and rightly so. You may lose the ability to 'play' the voice at all.

Implosion – sending the voice into yourself, creating resonance, using the space behind you to bounce the sound forward and seeing your audience

"I accept all that, but I can't believe that talking to myself, stuffing the vowel into my chest and imploding consonants is the whole picture. How do you *communicate*? How does that person - those three people - those 80 people know I am talking to them? How does the passion I have for what I say go to them? "

Look at the next diagram. How does this big fish get his dinner? Does he see it? Not down in the ocean where there is no light. He feels it. He feels the vibration through the water from the little fish. If he felt the same vibration on the whole of his body he would still not know which way to swim to approach them 'mouth first'. So the skin on the head of the fish is especially sensitive. It picks up the vibration and turns the fish towards his dinner. The mouth then only has to open.

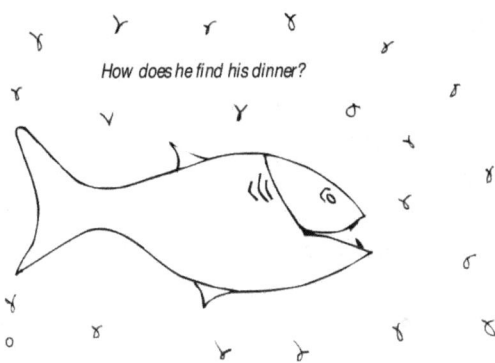

The performer and the audience

We have this sensitive facial area, handed down through evolution from our watery ancestors. We like to stroke this area of the face and to frequently touch it. We do not let anyone else touch this area until there is a close familiarity. It does not include the jaw or lower lip and chin, but begins under the nose and extends upwards and outwards. Where have you seen 'upwards and outwards' before? In the idea of spreading the soft palate at the back of your mouth (Chapter 7) and lifting the upper face to free the jaw to translate (Chapter 9).

This area is about taking in information, not about giving it out. This area monitors whether we are communicating with the audience or not. We receive information from the olfactory bulbs for smell; the eyes for vision; the nose breathing system of nostrils and sterilizing and warming nasal passages; the ears on the edge of this area for listening. Look at your face in the mirror— talk/sing to yourself.

The Efficient System of Communication, one-to-one, or one to a Multitude

You open communication with something simple and quite meaningless to make contact. "How are you?" "I am here to talk about..." Everyone has some meaningless phrases, some personal openers. Meanwhile you are absorbing the vibrations, the look and feel of the person/people before you, be they one or two thousand. You watch for their reaction to the things you say. Moment by moment their reaction may change and this tells you how to present your material, point-by-point, and moment-by-moment. You look, listen and feel the reaction to what you say, keeping each vowel sound well within you so that you listen to *yourself* first.

The sound that resonates within you travels along the Eustachian tubes, which connect the ear and the throat and you hear the total sound you make before anyone else hears it. Although the time factor is negligible, nevertheless this is a major factor in your self confidence when talking to others. You hear and check everything before it goes from you. People who are listening can be in front, to the side, or even outside the room, but they will hear some of the sound that radiates in all directions. When you work with 'implosion' you hear it all so don't be surprised if your voice begins to sound louder to you when you begin to work with this information. You need to get used to it by reading aloud and to accept that the loudness you hear is radiating outwards 360°. No one but you hears all of it.

Practice with other people's material

Use other people's passionate language and rhythm patterns for practice presentations. They are invaluable for getting used to the sound of your own voice. Get down to the library and discover some poets and prose writers. This includes singers. Enjoy the reading of poetry and stories to a few friends after dinner. This opens up:

- A feeling for what you say
- Passion in your voice when you need it
- Playing with dialect: give your poems a regional accent
- Speaking other languages: begin by reading in another language - maybe you learned one at school and haven't tried it since.

11. A Professional Voice for Life

Currently, in many professional vocal fields such as the management of people, directorship of companies, company training, professional singing, teaching, lecturing, free lance actors for TV and radio, as long as the voice appears to be working and doing everything you want it to, maintenance of the instrument itself does not seem to be an issue. Imagine having the same attitude to your car or your hot water system.

To develop and take care of your voice there are two separate tasks. One relates to the voice itself and the other to the material you 'play' on the voice.

1. Learn to play the instrument - and be sure you know exactly how it operates
2. Use your voice with as much variety of material, style and pitch range as possible.

Make a personal commitment to continue the development of both of these areas and do not hand the responsibility for your voice over to anyone else. You may get help or advice from teachers but you need to check out everything they say because only you are ultimately responsible for the care of your voice and only you are going to suffer if it deteriorates through poor handling.

The questioning adult mind should not launch into a potentially self-destructive activity like singing or speaking in public because someone, however apparently expert says, "Do it this way and it will be OK". You must check everything. Everything that you take on board must be both practical and research based. If the instructor cannot both explain *and demonstrate* all suggested changes simply and to your complete understanding and satisfaction, drop the instructor. After all, when you are up there singing, presenting, managing or lecturing, you are alone and 'free falling out of an aeroplane'. At that moment y*ou* have to be in charge of the information. Then you will be confident and personally empowered. Ask questions all the time. There are no stupid questions. Look at the mind map on the next page. It represents a structured 'life plan' for your voice. This chapter explains that plan and how to make sure that it happens.

Keep Growing

This book provides fundamental information about the mechanics and development of the voice. This is intended to grab your interest in this vital part of you and increase your desire to take responsibility for it. That means doing some maintenance, but maintenance of the voice could not be more enjoyable. When did you last read a poem aloud to your self or to anyone else? To say "I don't like poetry" is like saying "I don't like food". There are so many different kinds of poetry written about everything you could possibly think of or feel, that you will very soon find something that appeals to you. There are some easily accessible bboks of poetry listed at the end of this book.

This book complements the *VoiceGym* Exercise programme, which is a complete development and maintenance programme for the voice. However, merely *buying* the *VoiceGym* pack will not achieve the understanding or the development. You have to make time and take responsibility for doing it. *VoiceGym* is simple, fun, and easy to do, therefore changes come fast. Beyond the decision to do it in the first place, you don't have to think or make decisions. Get out the tools, put on the CD, do the exercises, sing the songs, It provides a structure to support your enthusiasm and keep it alive.

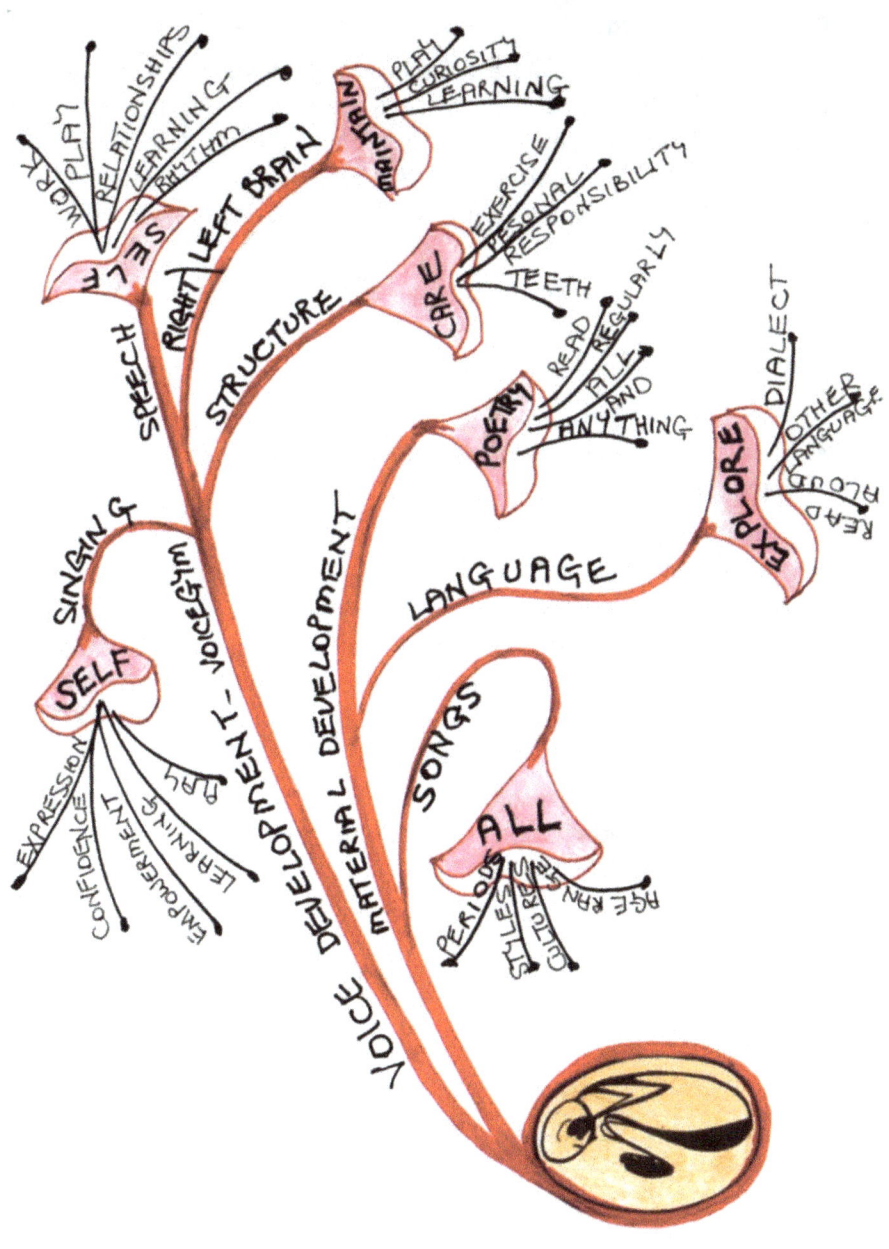

A Voice for Life

Even more Growth

Many good voices lose the plot because they develop only one aspect of the voice and then practice only the material within that narrow aspect. Career tracks can begin very early in life and this attitude appears to get very good results in the short term. A good voice will get you noticed. You may then be given opportunities that demand something different and original. But are you now -

- The singer who sounds like every other singer and has nothing different to say about the music this voice has been trained for?
- The entrepreneur who has an uninteresting, flat voice to present ideas with?
- The corporate company voice that gets stuck in corporate company jargon?
- The professional dealing with the public who fails to communicate with the patient or client?

All these people need to add variety to their vocal material to maintain maximum development of <u>specific</u> vocal skills. This has to include both speech *and* singing for everyone. We do not speak like Daleks; everything we say has pitch variety; everything we sing has words. We use the qualities of singing every moment in our speech.

Do you remember when someone you know and love walked in and said "Hello" and you thought "Oh dear, something is wrong"? The word did not tell you, but the pitch. Was it?

- A bit higher than usual, sounding tense?
- Down in the boots, sounding miserable?

And was the quality?

- Clipped and spat out from a tight throat through clenched teeth?
- Mumbled reluctantly with no welcoming smile?

Everyone uses language, pitch, colour, resonance and much more, both to express themselves and interpret the expression of others in

- different languages,
- different dialects within a language.

Mimicking other voices and characters is just the singing of different songs.

Professional speakers are sometimes appalled when I tell them there is no way to achieve the link between the information in your head, the thinking on your feet by which you climbed the company ladder, the ability to swing round on the press, meet the Channel 4 News reporter and come out without egg on your face if you don't sing.

"Singing is a musical talent. I'm not into music myself"

Singers are equally appalled at the thought of engaging with the audience and introducing themselves because 'on the fly' communication is not what has been practiced and prepared.

'Practiced and prepared' often exposes the lack of human communication left in a voice that has been stripped of everything except one channel of controlled sound.

Make sure you work on developing both the instrument itself and the material it 'plays' in both speech and singing, separately and by dovetailing them together.

Experiment

Learn a song. Panic! "I'm not a singer how do I do that?" Buy a song book with a CD where there are tracks with a voiceover that you can sing with and know when to come in while you follow the words. When you know a song all the way through and feel confident that you can use the copy merely for reference, put on the backing track without the voice over and

1. Speak the first phrase to the music
2. Sing the second phrase
3. Speak and sing the phrases alternately throughout the song.

If you are a singer and read music sing anything from your repertoire and do the same

There are four gains from attention to these two separate, linked areas of development:
- Increased listening skills
- Extension of pitch without
- Greater sense of rhythm
- Much better singing
- Greater enjoyment

Singing

I have managed to write *VoiceGym* Book without so far separating speech and singing and hopefully I have banged on about their interdependence for so long that consideration will be given to allowing them to develop and live together in *your* life, whatever the vocal agenda. At some point, however, if you are going to specialize in any professional skill you will have to move into a specialist training area, over and above any development encouraged or planned in this book.

The reality is that singing and speech <u>are</u> currently separated in specialist because all education and vocal training separates them from Day 1. There are singing lessons, drama lessons, speech therapists that do not sing, singing teachers who only deal with words in relation to music. Voice education and development needs to be rethought, but in the mean time we have to live by what is available and there is current methodology in the system that defeats the aim of 'a voice for life' in the general population.

Developing the voice by scales

Breathing exercises have been dealt with in Chapter 5 and I hope, unless you have some pathological reason for not doing so, you have given them up. The other fundamental in the training of singing based on 'received wisdom' is the use of the scale. Let's examine the scale as a voice-training tool.

Stewart Macpherson, in the 'Rudiments of Music', describes a scale as "An alphabetical succession of sounds having reference to some starting point, or key note. Counting from 'A' on a keyboard either up or down on the white keys: 'A, B, C, D, E, F, G', we eventually come back to 'A' again. The same can be done from 'B, C', or any other starting note. Progressing from any letter to the repeat of that letter and using each letter once we can produce an alphabetical succession of sounds having reference to some starting point, or key note".

But between those two sounds with the same name are eleven other different sounds, with only seven letters to name them. Which notes do you choose out of the possible eleven when you make up your 'alphabetical succession of sounds'? Instead of playing the white 'F', you could choose the black key to the right of it instead and completely change the progression.

Music of the world and of the concert hall contains an infinite variety of these 'alphabetical successions of sounds' making a variety of different scale patterns. The table on the next page identifies some of them. This is not a book to analyse musical forms. The point I make is

"Reader, if you have singing lessons, which scales do you sing?"

I bet you sing the ones in the top row and use them to warm up your voice, stretch your pitch range and train your ear for more acute listening to in-tuneness. In fact I would go as far as betting that you only sing the *major* ones. Unless, of course you are taking lots of singing exams, in which case you will do minor ones and in more advanced grades, even chromatic.

Am I also right in thinking that your repetitive exercises, practicing vowel sounds, are also based on the diatonic scale? None of this has the remotest relevance to the stretching of voice pitch range, or the development of the colour and resonance of the instrument. It is all to do with the music we play. This is borne out by the inability of singers whose voices are trained on singing scales, to improvise, or to sing music of a broad range of styles. If you train the voice to sing diatonic scales then that is the kind of music you will be most comfortable singing because the voice/brain relationship will be driven into that particular musical channel. Add the tonality regularly used in jazz, pop, modern music or folk music and the voice and brain are panicking.

Scales have an important place in musical training, but not in voice development. Excessive work on the purity, beauty and tuning of the voice itself simply using vowel sounds disconnects the voice from the colours and sonorities the composer has in mind for the language he has chosen. An excessive attention to the beauty of your own personal sound risks placing your ego between the music and the experience the audience is entitled to.

Where	When	What Scales
Classical music – Mozart, Haydn, Beethoven	Written approximately 1750-1850	Diatonic major and minor
Chopin	Mid 19th Century	Chromatic
Debussy	Late 19th Century – early 20th Century	Whole tone
Modernists	Late 20th-21 Century	Atonal – any arrangement
Jazz, Swing and its numerous offspring	Late 19th Century	Varieties of all previous scales
Folk music and pop	Always	Modal, sometimes not even using all 7 letters

Producing any sound with the voice is an involuntary action concerning ear and right brain, which hear (imagines) the sound. The laryngeal mechanism processes the instructions. Pitch is not 'a note we call Bb'. The tuning depends on listening not just to that pitch but the bright or dull quality of that pitch *in relation to the vowel within a particular language and the meaning it is expressing.*

Your ear does not select the pitch sounds you desire to sing from scales, but the chord progressions *from which the scales are formed*

All the scales in the columns above are formed from the harmonic progressions (chords) that colour and differentiate between the styles, periods and musical structures of the music. The voice and the ear extend and develop musical repertoire from

- the harmony, not the melodies,
- the chords, not the scales.

This presents a major shift in most belief systems, along with tongue position (Chapter 6) and the dangers of over breathing (Chapter 5).

Everything that encourages improvisation encourages accurate listening and pitch extension.

First discover the extent of the pitch you already can sing without outside musical stimulation. Sing the verbs and speak the rest in any piece of writing.

We can represent speech as a wave because it varies in pitch. Singing pitch can be either above or below the range of speech pitch:

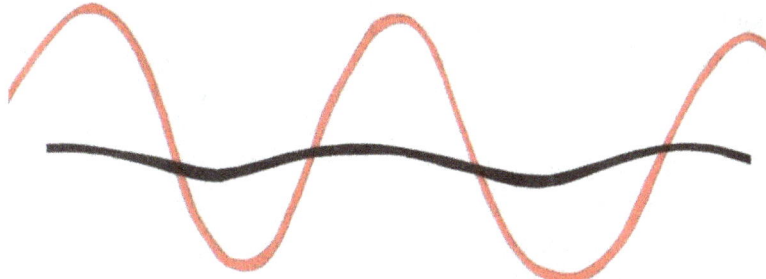

The black line represents speech, red is singing. Singing pitch goes much higher than speech, but also much lower. Extend means to move in any direction, but most vocal exercises only ascend. Why is that?

If you are one of the people for whom speech and singing are in two separate voices your belief about the way singing works may have, over the years, raised the pitch of your speaking voice. Allow total flexibility. Throw away learned parameters. There may be something wonderful to be gained by joining them together. Improvisation will also connect both speech and singing pitch to the sonorities of more accurate tuning

Improvise to chord progressions to extend pitch range

When investigating scale patterns we played around with the keyboard from 'A' - find the one nearest to your left hand – through all the letters 'B, C, D, E, F, G' to the 'A' above. If you sing the 'A' under your left hand the easiest sound for the voice to sing next is the next 'A' above it. That looks a long way on the keyboard, but your voice does not work like a keyboard. Unfortunately most of the introduction to singing in schools in western culture involves a keyboard and scales. We come to believe that there are seven other sounds to climb over if we want to sing a low 'A' followed by the one above.

'A to A' on the keyboard is called an octave: 'oct' meaning 8. These are the simplest progressions for the voice, counting on the keyboard –

1-8, followed by (not in order) 1-5, 1-6, 1-3, 1-4, 1-flattened 7th (b7th)

If you roll on the floor, stretch in spirals and improvise to any backing track you select, these are the musical intervals (one sound followed by another) that your voice will most easily sing in response to any backing track of chord progressions. The voice sings these pairs easily because both sounds belong to the same harmonic series. All we have to do to encourage the ear/brain/voice to play around with this pattern, sing more notes in the series in an upward or downward direction and we extend the voice. Notice the absence of 1-2, which would be the next sound in a scale, but does not belong to a simple chord. 1-2 is the hardest progression for the voice to sing in tune because these notes have no harmonic connection, yet 1-2 is the beginning of every major diatonic scale generally used in 'received wisdom' to train of the voice.

The rest is achieved by maintaining body balance and stretch, then just letting the voice 'go' with the music. Stretch in twists and spirals. Couldn't be easier.

- Roll on the floor to maintain perfect balance (drop the head at all times).
- Roll in twists and rotations to stretch the whole body
- Sing phrases allowing the vowels to move across pitch as the chords direct – and they will.
- Begin extending the voice by going for the next available sound while at full stretch with a big smile. It will probably be the octave.
- Don't stop there. Swing onto the next available sound – it may be the 5th above that.
- Go into descending pitch, letting your voice spring down to the next sound as the chords give you the lead. You must stretch to do this too.
- Singers! Put on the backing track of a song or aria, something fast and rhythmic (Handel – with runs?). Roll <u>slowly</u> and find how easy it is to sing runs fast, accurately and not run out of breath.

You will not believe the pitch range you will discover on the floor, well not at first, but the mere taste of what your voice will really do will send you back again and again to experiment. Experimenting with improvisation while rolling will discover your complete vocal range and give you the experience you can ultimately find when upright on two feet.

As pitch extends and confidence in ability to sing that range also extends, songs take on the aspect of 'what do I want to say'. That is, the song begins to develop from the words. This is much more enjoyable than using music as some sort of personal challenge where you win if you manage to sing the whole song through and not chicken out of the 'top note at the end'.

If you sing ascending scales and exercises, it will inevitably become an exercise in how high you can sing. The end of range then becomes an ego trip.

"I sang a top C today. It was a bit of a struggle, but I made it. I've never sung a top 'C' before". The use of the voice gravitates to:

- working the body without thought or imagination
- sitting for hours in pursuit of new ideas (much better go for a walk)
- working the voice without connecting it to the physical system that runs it
- singing endless vowels to achieve a 'constant' in tone quality
- None of this is productive.

Thinking beyond what is available

After the first couple of years of school special lessons for singing are generally available, which always involve a piano. By the time the child is 10, singing is part of school music and the choir. The ability to repeat specific notes or tunes played on the piano becomes the test for whether or not one can sing (get into the choir). It is perceived that singing happens in the music room – speech happens everywhere else. The few good voices emerging from this system generally have singing lessons.

Singing cannot be taken on like a subject in school, where the examination goal is set and that directs the learning process. The voice is an internal instrument reflecting life development and experience. That life experience does not have to have dramatic aspects, just day-to-day events will do, but the voice needs to grow on what may be in some potentially good voices, a very difficult life. If you look at the lives of great people, their lives are often also tragedies. The voice that sings their work has to come from someone who understands something of what the composer felt. To attempt to connect personal experience and the work of great songwriters on a series of grade examinations testing purity of tone and correctness of notational detail is to miss the point and purpose of voice development into singing.

Ideally the order of learning to sing should begin with words, as in early development. An interest in language and its power to persuade on all levels leads naturally into a fascination for the way music can enhance words and the devices various songwriters use to create their individual interpretation. The real singer is above all a lover and respecter of words, language, literature and poetry: a verbal seducer. Pitch, resonance and variety of tone are precise tools with which to intensify that verbal seduction. Learning to paste words on melodies and sing them accurately and clearly is a miniscule part of singing.

Where singing works

Why have Italy, Russia and Wales produced so many singers for the 'World Stage'? Why does the black African make such a wonderful sound? The Italians, the Russians, the Welsh, the black Africans have the same mechanical 'bits' as everyone else in the world, but they also have languages with a rhythm that ensures the speaker lands on the vowel. They also use a much broader pitch band when they speak. They are more vocal cultures – they talk more. Their history gives them a lot to express and they don't store it – they voice it.

The importance of movement cannot be stressed enough. In cultures where good voices occur naturally, dancing comes before singing. The dancing begins to express an idea or a story, and as the rhythm creates physical excitement the singing begins.

When you have felt vowels resound in your chest from the moment your larynx arrived in its adult position at 6 years old, especially if you were carried on your mother's back and heard the rich adult voice resonating in her body, you are unlikely to lift the vocal suspension to sing. It feels comfortable right where it is, low in your pharynx. Singing is a natural inheritance if your home background and education system encourages a love of language by awakening an awareness of your literary and musical heritage.

Registers in the voice

The piano keyboard is about four feet long. This is to contain all the separate keys that have to be pressed to produce the separate sounds. The violin reduces this length by having four strings and using finger pressure to split them into separately vibrating sections. Thus the violin will fit between your chin and your bent arm. The Vocalis muscles that produce the enormous pitch range of the human voice are contained within a couple of rings of cartilage, a space of about 3 cm in diameter. Major mechanical shifts have to occur to produce this pitch range. Received wisdom encourages the control of this shift mechanism and much practice time is devoted to smoothing over the changes of sound that can be heard and felt in some instances. Learning a song can become an exercise in 'ironing', where the singer is consciously trying to integrate what are termed 'chest voice, middle voice and head voice'.

This shifting should not be felt any more than the different stages of digestion or circulation of the blood should be felt. Conscious control of pitch bands and resonance, like conscious control of the breathing system (where you find one control, the other is usually being applied) is effortful, limiting and can have no long-term success. When evolution develops the most advanced and complex tool of creation is it likely that the mechanical shifts necessary for its application would be left to humans to organise – especially as controlling the voice is also controlling the breathing system?

I first learned to drive in a 1929 Humber 16 with a 'crash' gearbox, a family inheritance after the Second World War. That meant every change of speed had to be anticipated, because the shift onto using the larger revolving gear wheel had to be precisely timed. There was then a procedure called 'double de-clutch' to be learned and if you got it all right the car picked up speed without the jerk that shot the back seat passengers onto the floor. That was not, however, their main danger, for while I was concentrating on all this, my eye left the road.

We have moved into the 21st century. There are now automatic gearboxes that think for you and change gear whenever the demand of the road ahead could be better served by a mechanical shift to change the ratio of speed to effort. There is less wear on the engine because the designer knows engineering possibilities the driver will never know and the computer under your bonnet is programmed to those specifications. You do not need to know which gear you are in. You just drive happily and easily along concentrating on where you want to go next.

You voice has the latest BMW automatic gearbox. Don't reduce it to a 'crash box':

- Maintain rotation and stretch
- Use all three constrictors for vowel articulation
- Don't over breathe
- Build styloglossus into a working muscle for efficient tongue position
- Begin with the words, not the tune

Your automatic gearbox will emerge from this advanced engineering and you will be able to abandon yet another conscious control.

The voice doesn't age, we collapse into flexion

The freely operating and well maintained voice reflects us absolutely. However, if we hide our emotional pain by avoiding thinking, feeling or expressing it then the voice will reflect that tension. By controlling our emotions and not communicating them the voice loses some of the ability to express the way we are. We limit our voices socially, emotionally and intellectually if we limit ourselves socially, emotionally and intellectually; if we fail to maintain physical flexibility, co-ordination and balance; if we stop running, jumping and skipping. Reduce the physical demand and the demand on the breathing system is also reduced. Inefficiency in the breathing system is inefficiency in the voice. A lack of intellectual curiosity limits the voice. A lack of desire to communicate limits the voice. Although there is no reason for any of this to occur with age, there is a tendency to believe that it must. When we stop extending ourselves, we cannot just stay as we are, we move into flexion, which reduces us in every way.

A voice thus limited will be lacking in rhythm and spring, it will be dull and flat and unattractive. The voice in this person will sound old. I have encountered old voices on 25year olds and voices in 66 year olds that make your hair stand on end with the magic, wit and humour expressed. When you hear singing that stops you in your tracks, the instrument is young and vital – at any age. If you always maintain flexibility and balance in body, brain and voice and the connections one with the other, there is no reason why singing and speech should not be exciting until all systems fail together and they nail you down. Think of all the famous last words....

There is another path to the old voice. If the voice is continuously subjected to overpressure through over breathing and conscious control of the diaphragm –compensatory muscle systems are co-opted to support what is a fundamentally unnatural system. These muscle systems can be co-opted in their capacity as emergency support but can have no long-term programme: they are merely propping up physical malpractice. To speak or sing do you

- Tighten muscles in the legs?
- Lock the knees?
- Tighten the buttocks (hold a bus ticket between them)?
- Fix the ribs?
- Brace your Rectus Abdominus muscle (I once sang with a tenor who prided himself that someone could stand on his solar plexus when he sang a top 'C'. I haven't heard of him for years – I expect he exploded!

You can do all this for so long and at first it will certainly get you the high notes in '1st Soprano', or fill the classroom, but sooner or later this emergency system will begin to give way. Voices connected to this unnatural system do not last for life. Singing is generally over by the mid forties because the pitch range is failing and speech is flat and dull. Failing professional communicators take early retirement. Sadly they then often teach!

Choirs

Age related voices are most noticeable in choral societies, where the first sopranos are in their 20s, the second sopranos slightly older. Altos begin late thirties and second altos are nearest to the exit door, because by mid forties the voice has a distinctly uncontrollable 'wobble'. If pitch range is dropping like this it is a sure sign that the pressure is reducing through compensatory muscle failure. But the pressure should not be there in the first place, nor should the compensatory muscle system.

Exceptions are those young female voices with a deep rich resonance, who are immediately placed in the altos because they are able to hold the second part of the four-part harmony. These are the *natural* singers, whose voices are *naturally* maturing and passing through a *natural* change of pitch perception between ear and voice. These voices are relatively stable because they have been allowed to find a natural pitch level – that is why they are so secure in singing a second line. Sadly these voices may be the real quality soprano voices, but choral singing demands a top line of a-sexual quality. Most of the music was written for either the treble (boy's unbroken voice) or the castrato (the male, surgically retained alto) neither of which displayed any emotion in the voice. Women who wish to match this sound must depress their female power and thus their woman's voice.

Men should have more chance of singing throughout life without losing voice quality or pitch range because in puberty boy's voices are more likely to be allowed to go through the process of change to adult. That is, of course, if they do go on singing. However, once again the choral tradition can interfere with this natural progression.

Boys are sometimes taken into the choral tradition via choral scholarships as early as 7 or 8. They are then trained in sight-reading and music skills that enable them to sing complicated music at sight. While this is an invaluable training for the language of music it retains the unbroken voice too far into puberty for natural progression to the male voice. The treble voice is kept firmly under pressure to maintain its 'purity' and when it finally gives way, the resulting tenor, baritone or bass is still singing on this artificial pressure system. It is rare for this man to recover natural singing and be able to sing for pleasure for life. Most trebles who have had a long singing life well into puberty fail to sing as adults, losing all they have gained by their early efforts. For those boys who merely sing in school singing will be dropped as the pitch perception is lost when the voice drops into a man's sound. Few school teachers know what to do with this stage, so the boy is often dropped out of voice related activities for a while. 'For a while' can easily become a lifetime.

Maintain the continuity

If all stages of voice development are encouraged and there is no 'retirement', of voice, brain and body at any age the voice will undergo the same changes as we undergo in other ways. The adult voice will continue to fulfil the demand of an ever questioning and curious brain to speak and sing as long as the brain is curious. Just don't expect it to be continuously beautiful. Like all other parts of us it has its off days too. Be kind to it, give it lots of good nutrition in the form of a varied repertoire and the results can be far reaching. Breathing, rhythm, balance on two feet, mental alertness, all continue while voice, body and brain still excite one another.

Conclusion

Singing has to grow and develop from language skills and physical and emotional stability. That is the bottom line message of the *VoiceGym Book*. Singing is also as important as speech, so sing regularly, anything that grabs you.

One day you will hear a grand song or aria and think, "I can sing that" because you have already found all the sounds through play, not through struggle. Listen until you know it in your head, and what you know in your head, your voice will sing. This is the way to sing pop, Schubert, operatic arias or anything else and it gives you an amazing feeling of personal power. You find the sounds inside yourself while running up a hillside and shouting with the sheer joy of getting to the top. When you hear them in Verdi's Othello, you recognise them and know already how to reproduce them. It is then just a matter of putting the pattern of the music into your head. The current generation has a great singing divide. There are a few great voices doing everything in the public arena but the majority of the population neither sings nor particularly enjoys language skills. To have only a small percentage of the population articulate in speech and singing is a social failure.

VoiceGym offers the possibility to wipe the slate of attitudes and assumptions and begin again. It is an opportunity to discover, play with, get to know and eventually understand the workings of your voice. You can then include it in your life, with all its potential and all its joy.

What Next?

A career in professional voice does not require you to change any of the principles you have learned here. The engine works the same, whatever the geography, whatever the level of demand. It may have to work harder, more efficiently, faster, or for longer, but engines wear when the driver fails to respect the need for maintenance and Tender Loving Care (TLC), not when they have to work hard.

The Voice, body and brain will do anything for you that it can. It is your system, designed for maximum development of your own potential. When you want to do things, it will pull out all the stops to provide the means for you. You have only to exercise voice, body and brain together and give it lots of fun things to do to get the best from it in every way.

Musical input

Always remain in charge of your own voice. Once you play the instrument well and you want to extend your singing further you will need lessons in musical style and repertoire. For this you need a singing coach or an accompanist. See useful Contacts. This is the stage where you will need to sing scales. To sing Bach, Handel or other composers of the Baroque period you have to speed up the whole vocal action by singing exercises based on the relevant scales used by the baroque composers. Rossini will require practice of specific ornaments used in his period. Jazz, pop, folk, rock, are all just styles of music with their own scales and musical architecture.

To sing the big stuff – opera, lieder, Russian, French or Italian song you will have to work for maximum vocal and physical flexibility and strength – lots of rolling improvisation stretching the pitch range and lots of listening to music in the style you want to sing. The rest is down good specifically guided body exercise with someone who understands the physical needs of performance. Multidirectional sport is also good; tennis, cycling, squash. Certainly you will have to build the external oblique muscles and strengthen the work of the pelvic floor. You need an expert to help with this.

Find someone who speaks the language of the songs you want to sing and trade ironing (?) for help with Russian, or an afternoon taking the kids out for help with that song cycle by Debussy. Both benefit, this is community music – the most productive kind.

However proficient you become at singing, the maintenance you have just learned must never be neglected. It is your base for everything you sing.

Speech Input

Have you ever considered reading plays to discover different character traits and anticipate behaviour from the dialogue? This can be great practice for doing the same in the workplace, in song and opera and in life.

Read the best in your own language aloud to yourself until you feel the buzz, then read it someone else and give him or her the same buzz. You may join a drama group, or speak in public and present because you *enjoy* it. Dinner parties can become occasions for storytelling, singing, and reading poetry aloud.

Find the joy in language and song. Everyone can have it. You just have to get to know your own voice. Don't miss out.

Appendix

Singing for children

Early VoiceGym

School no longer offers enough singing, so parents need to consider taking responsibility for children's voices and singing to ensure a confident voice in the young adult. **Early VoiceGym** is an exercise system based on a song book that contains a CD with voiceovers and backing tracks. There is a note book for parents explaining how to work with children using the song book and what each exercise is doing. The exercises are in the form of games to make it fun. There is a DVD of children working with the programme, to give parents confidence that they have the right approach. School teachers can use **Early VoiceGym** for class work and it also covers reading aloud, improves posture and confidence. Anyone doing this with children will also improve their own voice.

Early VoiceGym is available from www.voicegym.co.uk

Song Books

The following are song books published by A & C Black, London. The songs are sung by very natural voices accompanied by simple instruments like flutes, drums, whistles, bells etc. Any adult with a sense of fun can take a child through these songs. Children's voices develop best from natural sound, especially that of other voices. If the family sings, the child will also sing.

Books with cassettes/CDs available separately:

   Okki-tokki-unga: Book - 0 7136 4078 2; Double cassette - 0 7136 4081 2

   Apusskidu: Book - 0 7136 4437 0; Double cassette - 0 7136 4438 9

   Banana splits: Book - 0 7136 4196 7; CD - 0 7136 4650 0

   Ta-ra-ra boom de-ay: Book - 0 7136 1789 6; CD - 0 7136 5936 X

   Sing a Christmas cracker: Book - 0 7136 5160 1, CD - 0 7136 5788 X

Books with CD included:

   High low Dolly Pepper - 0 7136 3329 8

   Game songs with Prof Dogg's Troupe - 07136 6207 7

Sing hey diddle diddle - 0 7136 5934 3
Carol, gaily carol - 0 7136 5794 4
Harlequin - 0 7136 6240 9
Someone's singing Lord - 0 7136 6344 8
Everyone's singing Lord - 0 7136 6372 3
The Singing Sack - 0 7136 5805 3
Mango Spice - 0 7136 6097 X
Sonsense nongs - 0 7136 5935 1
Merrily to Bethlehem - 0 7136 6751 6
Flying around - 0 7136 6343 X
Strawberry Fair - 0 7136 5832 0
Sing a silver lining - 0 7136 6355 3

Singing for adults

VoiceGym

Fundamental exercise materials and other essential tools for voice work in singing or speech with teenagers and adults. The exercises are all very simple and are explained clearly and with photographs. You can improve your voice by yourself with this system if you follow the simple instructions and practice regularly.

Other Resources

Many albums of songs are being re-issued with backing tracks of 'across the board' repertoire. You can sing with some top accompanists and good live bands, which helps you with musical style and speed. Operatic arias come with orchestral accompaniment. Search the internet for those with a voice over version that you learn from as well as a backing track where you can sing by yourself.

Book a couple of hours with someone who reads music (useful contacts) to mark copies so that you know where to come in and how to read signs on the music. Always learn it by listening.

Remember, you must do the exercises, songs and poems *with* children if they are to do and enjoy them.

Learning to Read and Improving your Reading Aloud

- Always have a music stand or a table stand at the right height for you to look straight ahead. Print pages for practice in a large font.
- Use a long pointer to trace where the eye must travel. Place it below the line of words and move it slowly *but continuously.* Do not stop on the words.
- Poetry is divided into lines for its rhythm structure, much like music is divided into bars and phrases but ends of lines are not necessarily stopping places. Imagine the pictures and wrap the lines to fit the pictures.

Useful Contacts

Functional Orthodontics

The following two organisations carry lists of dentists and orthodontists who network with other clinical disciplines

Society for the Study of Cranio-mandibular Disorders
www.jawache.com

The Cranio Group
www.craniogroup.com

Chiropactors and Osteopaths

The Osteopathic Centre for Children, London
www.occ.uk.com

The Sutherland Society – the UK organisation for cranial osteopathy
www.cranial.org.uk

The British Chiropractic Association

www.chiropractic-uk.co.uk

CHEK

CHEK practitioners offer nutrition, metabolic typing, exercise, and lifestyle management for optimum health and well being.

www.chekconnect.com

Natural birthing

The Active Birth Clinic
25 Bickerton Road, London, N19 5JT
020 7281 6760
www.activebirthcentre.com

Work with early reflex patterns

The Institute for Neuro Physiological Psychology (INPP)
1 Stanley Street, Chester CH1 2LR
01244 311 414
www.inpp.org.uk

Natural Breathing for Health

Buteyko Therapy
www.buteyko.com

Children's Summer Music Camps

ShareMusic South-West
www.sharemusicsouthwest.org

Jazz workshops, books and training systems

Jamey Aebersold (an American company, but see website for UK dealers)
www.jazzbooks.com

Musicians/teachers/accompanists

www.musicteachers.co.uk

Each County Education Department has a 'Music Services' Department holding lists of music teachers in the area.

For Reading Poetry Aloud and enjoying it

Blazing Fruit by Roger McGough, Published by Penguin. ISBN 0-14-058652-0.

The Way Things Are by Roger McGough. Published by Penguin. ISBN 0-140-28632-2.

A Survival Kit for Modern Life to get you through the Day (and night) edited by Daisy Goodwin. Published by Harper Collins. ISBN 0-00-710650-5.

101 poems to keep you Sane – emergency rations fpr the seriously stressed. edited by Daisy Goodwin. Published by Harper Collins ISBN 0-00 712796-0.

Bibliography and References

References in books

Alexander F.M. (1932) *The Use of the Self*. Methuen & Co., London. ISBN 0-575-03820-2

Ames L. (1967) *Is Your Child in the Wrong Grade?* Harper and Rowe, New York.

Arnold A. (1995) *Rhythm and Touch, an Introduction to Craniosacral Therapy*. Brotherhood of Life Publishing, Alberquerque NM. ISBN 0-914732-35-8

Brown O. (1996) *Discover Your Voice, How to Develop Healthy Voice Habits*. Singular Publishing Group, San Diego CA. ISBN 1-56593-704-X

Bunch M. (1993) *The Dynamics of the Singing Voice*. Springer-Verlag, Wien. ISBN 0-387-82394-8

Buzan T. (1982) *Use Your Head*. BBC Books, London. ISBN 0 563 16552

Caine A. (1991) *The Voice Workbook, Use your Voice with Confidence*. Hodder and Stoughton, London. ISBN0-340-54215-2

Caine A. (1998) Voice Therapy. In *Complementary Therapies in Dental Practice*, ed. Peter Varley. Butterworth-Heinemann, Oxford. ISBN 0 7236 1035 9

Chek Paul. (2004)Eat, *Move and be Healthy*. C.H.E.K. Institute San Diego, CA, USA. ISBN: 1-58387-006-7

Crelin E.S. (1987) *The Human Vocal Tract, Anatomy, Function, Development, Evolution*. Vantage Press, New York. ISBN 0-533-06967-X

Crosby E.C. Humphrey T. and Lauer E. (1962) *Correlative Anatomy of the Nervous System*. The Macmillan Co., NY.

Curtis B. Jacobson S. and Marcus E. (1972) *An Introduction to the Neurosciences*. W.B. Saunders & Co., Philadelphia.

Faiz O. & Moffat D.(2003) *Anatomy at a Glance*. Blackwell Science. ISBN 0-632-05934-6

Fink R. and Demarest R. (1978) *Laryngeal Biomechanics*. Harvard University Press.. ISBN 0 – 674 51085-2

Fonder A. (1990) *The Dental Distress Syndrome*. Medico-Dental Arts, Rock Falls IL.

Gänzl K. (1995) *The complete story of stage musicals*. Smithmark Publishers, New York. ISBN 0-8317-1890-0

Goddard S. (2002) *Reflexes, Learning and Behaviour, a Window into the Child's Mind*. Fern Ridge Press OR. ISBN 0-9615332-8-5

Guyton A. (1977) *Basic Human Physiology: Normal Function and Mechanisms of Disease*. Saunders Company, Philadelphia, PA. ISBN 0-7216 4383-3.

Hiatt J. and Gartner L. (1987) *Textbook of Head and Neck Anatomy*. Williams and Williams, Baltimore MD. ISBN 0-683-03975 – X.

Howat J. (1999) *Chiropractic, Anatomy and physiology of Sacro Occipital Technique*. Cranial Communications Systems, Oxford. ISBN 0 9537286 0 9

Kapandji I. (1974) *The Physiology of the Joints*. Churchill-Livingstone, Edinburgh. ISBN 0-443-01209-1

Kawamura Y. (1968) Mandibular Movement . In *Facial Pain and Mandibular Dysfunction*. eds. L. Schwartz and C. M. Chayes. Saunders & Co. Eastbourne.

McCallion M. (1988) *The Voice Book*. Faber & Faber, London. ISBN0-571-15059-4.

Macdonald G. (1999) *Complete Alexander Technique, a Practical Programme for Health, Poise and Fitness*. Paragon, Bath. ISBN1-84164-163-4.

McDevitt E (1989) *Functional Anatomy of the Masticatory System*. Butterworth, London. ISBN 0-7236-1523-3

Mc Manus C. *Right Hand, Left Hand*. .Phoenix,UK. ISBN 0-7538-1355-6

Macpherson S. (1939) *Rudiments of Music*. Galliard, New York. ISBN 852 49010 0.

Myers Thomas.(2001) *Anatomy Train*. Churchill Livingstone ISBN0 443 06351 6

Page D. (2003) *Your Jaws – YourLife*. SmilePage Publishing, Baltimore MD. ISBN0-9717368-1-2.

Odent M. (1984) *Birth Reborn*. Souvenir Press, London.

Pickney C. (1988) *Callanetics for Your Back*. Callan Ebury Press, London. ISBN 0-85223-912-2.

Platzer W. (1992) *Locomotor System, Color Atlas/ Text of Human Anatomy, Vol 1*. Thieme Verla,Stuttgart, Germany. ISBN3-13-533304-3.

Robertson L. and Thompson G. (1998) *Body Control the Pilates Way*. Pan Books,London. ISBN 0330 369458.

White G. and Forest A. (1981) *Double Yoga, A New System for Total Body Health*. Penguin Books Ltd., UK. ISBN 0 14 046 505 7.

References in Papers and Journals

Caine A. (1995) Beyond chewing. *Cranio-View: The Journal of the Cranio Group and the Society for the Study of Craniomandibular Disorders*, 4(4), 33-41.

Caine A. (1997) Voice: the forgotten fitness factor. *Positive Health*, December.

Caine A. (1998) Voice loss in performers: a pilot treatment programme to test the effect on the voice of correcting structural misalignment. *Logopedics, Phoniatrics and Vocology*, 23(Suppl.1), 32-37.

Caine A. (1998) Not only canaries need sing. *The Therapist: the Journal of the European Therapy Studies Institute*, 5(2), 10-14, Spring.

Caine A. (1999) Voice Therapy and Dentistry (with Peter Varley). *Dentistry Monthly*, April, 24-29.

Dart R. (1968) Voluntary Musculature in the Human Body, The Double Spiral Arrangement. *Human Potential,* Vol 1. No.2

Henderson Y. (1940) The History of Carbon-dioxide. Excerpt from *Cyclopedia of Medicine.*

Lum L. C. (1975) Hyperventilation: the Tip and the Iceberg. *Journal of Psychosomatic Research.* Vol 19. pp. 375-383.

Zenker W. and Zenker A. (1960) On the Regulation of the Vocal Folds through the Extrinsic suspension Mechanism (in German). *Folia Phonatrica*, 12, 1-36.

Glossary

Alveoli	Thin-walled chamber in the lung.
Anterior	Front.
Amphibian	Living on both land and in water.
Biped	Walking on two feet.
Branchial arches	Developments in the embryo at 6-7 weeks that form the bone structure of the face, mandible and Hyoid.
Bruxing	Teeth grinding.
Buccinator	The main muscle of the cheek, (the trumpet muscle).
Central Nervous System (CNS)	Composed of the brain and spinal cord.
Cerebro-spinal fluid (CSF)	Fluid that bathes the brain and spinal cord and cushions the CNS.
Cervical spine	First seven vertebrae – the neck.
Condyle	Thickened end of the mandible that forms one part of the TMJ.
Cranium	The skeleton of the head, without mandible or facial bones.
Dead Space	All air spaces between the nasal sinuses and the lungs.
Diaphragm	Dome-shaped sheet of skeletal muscle separating thorax and abdomen.
Dural port	Exit from the spinal cord for the spinal nerves.
Dural sleeve	Protective sheath covering the spinal nerve.
Epiglottis	Elastic cartilage (lid) at the top of the larynx: able to close, separating the airway from the pharynx.
Embryo	The earliest stage of human development 7-9 weeks after conception.
Eustachian Tube	The tube connecting ear and pharynx, pumped by the action of tongue/soft palate co-ordination in singing. Location of middle ear infection(glue ear).
Foetus (fetus)	The organism from the third month of development.

Glossary

Gravity	Force attracting all matter to the centre of the earth.
Hard palate	Bony roof of the mouth.
Homo Sapiens	Modern human species, developed 100,000 years ago.
Hyoid bone	Horse-shoe shaped bone suspended under the mandible from which the larynx is suspended.
Infrahyoid muscles	Suspensory muscle attachment to the hyoid from below.
Intercostal muscles	Small muscles attached between ribs and arranged to provide maximum flexibility in breathing..
Involuntary muscle	Smooth muscle, contracting without conscious control.
Larynx	Organ that produces the voice, made up of the, thyroid and Cricoid cartilages: the top two rings of the trachea.
Lateral Pterygoid	Muscle rising from facial bone and inserting into the capsular disc of the TMJ.
Obicularis Oris	The muscle round the lips, causing them to pout: the anterior sphincter of the gut.
Occiput	The rocker joint where the skull balances on the first vertebrae of the spine.
Peristalsis	The continuous wave movement of the smooth muscle of the gut.
Pharynx	The whole length of the three constrictors of the throat.
Primitive reflexes	Fetal and infant involuntary movement patterns and the entire physiological process activating them.
Proprioception	All sensations involving body position, whether at rest or in motion.
Pterygoid raphe	The fibrous moveable junction between Buccinator and the superior constrictor of the Pharynx that allows repositioning of both muscles according to function.
Reptilian	Stage of development of creeping, as in alligators, repeated in the early development of infants before crawling.

Rooting reflex	The early infant reflex to purse the lips: important to clinging and sucking.
Sacrum	The fused connection between spine and pelvis, shaped like an arrow and ending in the coccyx.
Sinus	A hollow cavity, as in the spaces behind the nose that contain air.
Soft palate	The muscular continuation of the hard palate important and active in breast feeding, breathing and articulation
Sacral tubercle	Anchor in the sacrum for the end of the dural tube, which contains the cerebro-spinal fluid.
Styloglossus	The muscle connecting the tongue up and back to the styloid process of the temporal bone
Supra-Hyoid Muscles	The muscles suspending the hyoid from the styloid process of the Temporal bone of the skull.
Tactile tissue	Smooth muscle tissue sensitive to touch, as in the inside of the mouth
Temporalis muscle	Muscle covering the temporal bone, the anterior part assisting in translation of the mandible
Temporo-mandibular Joint (TMJ)	The joint between mandible and temporal bone of the skull.
Thoracic Spine	The twelve vertebrae to which the ribs attach.
Trachea	Wind pipe.
Translation	The sliding action of a joint.

www.ingramcontent.com/pod-product-compliance
Lightning Source LLC
Chambersburg PA
CBHW060341170426
43202CB00014B/2846